Roses in December

Marilyn Willett Heavilin

HARVEST HOUSE PUBLISHERS

EUGENE, OREGON

Unless otherwise indicated, all Scripture quotations are taken from the King James Version of the Bible.

Verses marked NASB are taken from the New American Standard Bible®, © 1960, 1962, 1963, 1968, 1971, 1972, 1973, 1975, 1977, 1995 by The Lockman Foundation. Used by permission. (www.Lockman.org)

Verses marked RSV are taken from the Revised Standard Version of the Bible, copyright © 1946, 1952, 1971 by the Division of Christian Education of the National Council of the Churches of Christ in the U.S.A. Used by permission. All rights reserved.

Verses marked NIV are taken from the HOLY BIBLE, NEW INTERNATIONAL VERSION®. NIV®. Copyright © 1973, 1978, 1984 by the International Bible Society. Used by permission of Zondervan. All rights reserved.

Verses marked NKJV are taken from the New King James Version. Copyright © 1982 by Thomas Nelson, Inc. Used by permission. All rights reserved.

Verses marked TLB are taken from The Living Bible, Copyright ©1971. Used by permission of Tyndale House Publishers, Inc., Wheaton, IL 60189 USA. All rights reserved.

Cover by Left Coast Design, Portland, Oregon

Cover photo © Comstock Images / Alamy

Roses in December
Copyright © 1987 by Marilyn Willett Heavilin
Published by Harvest House Publishers
Eugene Oregon 97402

Library of Congress Cataloging-in-Publication Data

Heavilin, Marilyn Willett.
     Roses in December / Marilyn Heavilin.
          p. cm.
     Originally published: Nashville : T. Nelson, ©1993. With new appendices.
     Includes bibliographical references.
     ISBN-13: 978-0-7369-1779-7 (pbk.)
     ISBN-10: 0-7369-1779-9 (pbk.)
     1. Consolation.   2. Suffering—Religious aspects—Christianity.   3. Heavilin,
     Marilyn Willett.   4. Christian biography—United States.   I. Title.
BV4905.2.H455 2006
248.8'66—dc22   2005028093

Printed in the United States of America

06 07 08 09 10 11 12 13 14 /DP-KB/ 10 9 8 7 6 5 4 3 2 1

In memory of
Jimmy, Nathan, and Ethan,
three beautiful flowers
in my bouquet of
December Roses.

To Glen,
Matt and Debbie,
Mellyn and Mike.
Your love and encouragement
have kept me going.

Contents

A Note from the Author

Dear Reader,

When I first wrote *Roses in December* in 1985–86, it was impossible for me to imagine how others would respond to the book. I simply knew I had to write—for me, for my family, to keep the memory of my three sons alive, and for a more practical reason, to help me work through my own grief.

I was still too new in my grief to realize how universal my reactions were. Now, many years later, while I am pleased, I have learned not to be surprised when people tell me they identify so completely with me as I describe my own personal grief process.

When our son Nathan was killed by a drunk driver, I shouted to God through my pain, "Don't let this be wasted. It has to count. It must matter that Nathan, Jimmy, and Ethan Heavilin lived and that they died. Please don't let their lives be wasted."

A few years ago my husband and I were workshop leaders at a national convention of The Compassionate Friends, a support group for bereaved parents. It had been five years since we had spoken at a convention, so this was the first time we were able to receive many comments regarding *Roses in December*.

The first evening a woman walked up to me and said, "I can't believe I'm getting to meet you. I'm alive because of you!"

Naturally that caught my attention. She started to tell me her story, and it overwhelmed me. I asked her to write it out so I could share it with others, and she happily obliged.

I lost my only child Lisa on December 8, 1987. She died on her way to school, a passenger in a car driven by her 'best friend.' We received no support from her friend or her parents—someone told us they were afraid we would sue. We lived in Pennsylvania where my husband was stationed in the Marines, but our home was in Charleston, West Virginia. We took Lisa home for the last time!

When we got back to Pennsylvania, we had no family, no Lisa, no friends. Each day I wanted less and less to live. All our plans and dreams died with Lisa, as well as did my future—my grandchildren—all of it! I tried to talk my husband into a double suicide or a murder and suicide. How could we go on, or want to?

On a trip to West Virginia my dad took me to a Christian bookstore and bought me your book, *Roses in December*. I'm sure he wanted me to have it because Lisa loved roses, and she died in December.

I read the book in one sitting. The next day I read it again. Finally I had found a friend who understood and shared my feelings! I felt you knew my heartache of losing my only child because of your one-on-one relationship to your Nathan who died on February 10—my Lisa's birthday! My Lisa died in December; your Nathan was born in December.

How it must have hurt for you to have to go to work at the school without Nathan there—I couldn't even drive by Lisa's school. How wonderful that you wrote a book for me out of your grief for Nathan. I felt for the first time that my feelings were normal. I would grieve forever, but it was OK.

On the anniversary of Lisa's death we sent a rose to my parents and my five brothers and sister with the message, 'God gives us memories so we might have Roses in December.' They each took their rose that cold, sad day and put it on her grave since we were in Pennsylvania and couldn't be there for her. She will not be forgotten.

Thank you for your love. You saved my life with your compassion and caring!

Evelyn Ralston

During that convention I heard numerous comments similar to Evelyn's. Many said, "You gave me hope when I didn't want to live." Others stated, "We had hope for our marriage after we read *Roses in December.*"

As I listened to each story, I heard God whisper in my ear, "It wasn't wasted. It matters that they lived and that they died."

This past summer my husband Glen, our son Matthew, and I were the opening speakers for the International Conference of The Compassionate Friends in Philadelphia. Just before we spoke, a sparkly and smiling woman came up to me and said, "Do you remember me? I'm Evelyn!" After talking with her, I asked Evelyn to send me the postscript to her story.

On December 8th, the anniversary of our Lisa's death, the saddest day of every year for us, we received a phone call from my sister in West Virginia. She told us of a baby boy who was to be born and needed to be adopted. His birth mother was told of our loss of Lisa and the love we had for her. This birth mother then felt in her heart that she wanted us to have her baby!

Frank and I could only believe that receiving this news on such a sad day was truly a gift from God. The baby was not due until March, but can you believe he was born for us on February 14, 1995—exactly 25 years to the day we were given our Lisa—Valentine's Day, 1970, a day meant for love. We knew in our hearts Lisa would be very happy for us.

Marilyn, the love and encouragement we received from your book, *Roses in December,* gave us the strength to face the future and deal with our emptiness. Frank and I became leaders of the Wyoming Valley Chapter of The Compassionate Friends of Northeastern Pennsylvania. We found by helping others we were helping ourselves.

Even though parts of our hearts will always be broken, the realization of how precious life is and the compassion we've learned will guide us in the days ahead with our little son, Lee Franklin Ralston II, the little boy who calls us Mommy and Daddy.

Over 75,000 copies of *Roses in December* have been sold since its release in 1987. When my publisher asked that I update the book, I read through it and realized very few changes needed to be made. My story hasn't changed, and my observations and opinions regarding the grief process have been confirmed over and over. I have included some recent comments from those who have read the book or heard me speak, and I have updated personal information when it was pertinent. I have also related some experiences our family has had in the past few years, and my son Matthew has contributed a chapter on sibling grief.

The facilitator at The Compassionate Friends chapter we often attended opened the meeting by saying, "I am sorry each of you has a reason for coming here, but I am glad you have a place to come." May I paraphrase that statement to say, I am so sorry you have a need to read *Roses in December,* but since you do, I am grateful that such a book is available. I am comforted in knowing my grief has not been wasted.

September 2005....Well, here we are, getting ready for another update of *Roses in December*! Who could possibly have predicted that 18 years after its first publication, this little book would still be helping so many people deal with the loss of a loved one. Each day I'm more in awe of what God had in mind when I first sat down to that computer and poured my heart out to others who were experiencing the same pain I had gone through. Now I have had the privilege of meeting thousands of you, and I have you in mind as I'm reading through this manuscript.

Keep looking for the roses!

Your friend and fellow sufferer,
Marilyn Willett Heavilin

The Rose of Preparation

Even when walking through the dark
valley of death I will not be afraid, for
you are close beside me,
guarding, guiding all the way.

PSALM 23:4, TLB

I sat across the table from my friend Mary, silently sipping tea, waiting for her to speak. Her son had died just two weeks before. She started to speak several times, but her words were choked back by her sobs. Finally she took a deep breath and blurted out, "No one understands my grief. I feel so alone."

If you have recently experienced a heartbreak, you undoubtedly are well acquainted with feelings of isolation and loneliness. It is true that no one else can understand your grief completely or feel your individual pain, but I have experienced loss. I've lived through my own grief: the disappointments, the shattered dreams, the fears, the depression, and the emotional pain that made my whole body ache. I remember feeling, too, that no one else could possibly understand, but I've discovered it is possible to walk through that long, cold winter season of grief and emerge on the other side a whole, healthy person.

Dear friend, you don't have to go through your grief alone. Please let me join you in this winter season and share my very special December roses with you. The first rose along our path is the rose of preparation.

It was a cold, blustery February evening in 1943 when my mom and I climbed aboard the Greyhound bus and I excitedly waved goodbye to my daddy. We were going to a small town in northern Michigan to visit my grandparents, my aunt and uncle, and best of all, my three-month-old cousin, Mary Beth. Now she would be old enough to respond to me. I could hardly wait. I'd been praying for a baby brother or sister as long as I could remember, but since my prayer hadn't been answered, I doted on cousin Mary Beth.

As soon as Grandpa lifted me from the bus steps, I asked, "When can we see Mary Beth?" and was very disappointed when he said I'd have to wait until morning. I climbed in bed with Grandpa and Grandma before dawn and asked, "Can we go now?"

As I gobbled down my breakfast, I saw my aunt and uncle's truck coming up the lane. I anxiously met them at the door, but though only an unsuspecting, innocent five-year-old, I knew something was wrong when I saw the pain on their faces. Mary Beth wasn't with them.

We all stood in that old farm kitchen with the snow piled high against the stone walls and windows, and my Uncle Louie began to explain. Mary Beth had suffocated in the night. She was dead. I can still hear my own screams as I ran across the lane to my great-grandmother's home. "My baby's dead! My baby's dead!"

My screaming must have torn at the breaking hearts of the adults, but no one reproved me. They just picked me up and hugged me, and we cried together.

The snowstorm had closed the roads from town to my aunt's house, and when Uncle Louie had called the coroner and undertaker, he was told they would have to wait for the snowplow—it could be hours before they arrived. Our family all drove to my aunt and uncle's cottage where a kind neighbor waited with Mary Beth's still form.

I insisted on seeing "my baby," and no one had the strength to resist me. She had been a beautiful child, but the black and blue blotches that come with suffocation had stolen her beauty. I didn't care—she was still my Mary Beth. I sat by the bed, stroked her hand, and talked to her. She felt like a china doll—so cold and unresponsive.

In those wintry hours my family was able to deal with their grief and to say goodbye privately to our sweet little Mary Beth. My fear of death waned as my mom explained that Jesus was taking care of Mary Beth and someday I would see her again. My fear of dead bodies lessened as I touched Mary Beth and realized she wasn't in that body anymore.

As a child, that was my first but not my last contact with death. By the time I reached twelve, my paternal grandparents, my great-grandmother, a thirteen-year-old cousin, and a seventeen-year-old cousin all had died. Even my Aunt Lucille and Uncle Louie died after their gas stove exploded, causing a flash fire. It was through that tragedy that I got my long-awaited little brother Walt—my parents adopted the youngest of Aunt Lucille and Uncle Louie's three orphaned children.

Death was no stranger to my family, but I don't look back to a childhood filled with tragedy and sad memories. I remember a family made strong through sorrow, a family with a tenacity that triumphed over troubles, a family that cried and laughed together.

After my husband Glen and I were married, we had three children, Matthew, Mellyn (our only girl), and Jimmy. Our life seemed ideal. Glen was an executive with General Motors; we had a new home, and we were on our way to a successful life.

Early one morning Glen went in to make a routine check on the children, but suddenly his voice penetrated my slumber, "Marilyn, call the doctor—Jimmy's gone."

With my heart pounding and my mind racing, I obediently called our personal friend and physician. "Tom, come quick, it's Jimmy!" But I knew Glen must be mistaken.

I quickly hung up the phone and raced into Jimmy's room in time to see Glen trying to breathe life into our young son. As my eyes fixed on Jimmy's lifeless form with black and blue blotches, I gasped, "Mary Beth!" The memories came tumbling back in a wave. Could this be happening again?

While waiting for the doctor, Glen and I knelt, with the baby still in his arms, and we prayed, "Jesus, please use this situation for Your honor and glory." The autopsy said "interstitial pneumonia." Today we would probably classify this as a crib death.

Jimmy died more than forty years ago, but as I write this account some scenes are still very vivid: the hurt I heard in my mother's voice as we called with the terrible news; the panic I felt later that day when the thought crossed my mind, I haven't fed Jimmy! and then the wave of grief as I realized Jimmy was dead; the feeling of rage mixed with overwhelming sadness that I experienced when I went into Jimmy's room and discovered that well-meaning friends had removed all of Jimmy's furniture and clothing without my knowledge or permission. I also recall dreading to meet people on the street or in the grocery store because I didn't want to answer the question, "How's your baby doing?"

Glen and I trusted the Lord and were able to go on with our lives, though it was hard when we were told, "You can still have lots of babies, and you'll probably forget all about this."

A year and a half later we were delighted with the doctor's announcement that we were going to have twins. I reasoned that God was "paying us back" for the child He had taken. It's amazing how we try to fit God into our mind-set.

Our identical twin boys, Nathan James and Ethan Thomas, were born on Christmas morning, 1965. What a celebration we had! I received dozens of phone calls and bouquets. We were sure the birth of twins would lessen the pain of Jimmy's death.

We took Nathan home on New Year's Eve, but Ethan needed to gain a little weight. Each day I checked on Ethan and his progress was good. But on the ninth day his weight began going down and he was lethargic. Specialists were called in: diagnosis—pneumonia; prognosis—not good.

I was angry at life and at God. What had we done to deserve this? We were strong Christians, actively serving the Lord, and we had accepted Jimmy's death without bitterness or anger. Was this our thanks?

I struggled with God all night, and the next morning as I read out of *Streams in the Desert,* I thought I had found my answer. The verse for that day was "Go thy way; thy son liveth" (John 4:50).

I called all of my friends. "I'm sure Ethan will be fine. I'm sure that's what this verse means." Once again I thought I had God all figured out, but that evening as I pressed my face against the nursery window and watched my dear little Ethan labor with each breath, God spoke to me very clearly. "Marilyn, I loved you enough to die for you; aren't you willing to trust Me with this child?"

In an attempt to get alone with God, I went into the bathroom in the private room the hospital had given us, locked the door, slumped to the floor, and cried out to God. "This isn't fair. We're good people, good parents, good Christians. Why should this happen to us?"

Once I had blurted out my feelings, I sat silently for a while and then a peace began to grow within me. My prayer continued, "Lord I don't understand this, and I certainly don't like it. But I love You and I trust You. I give You complete control over Ethan's life. Now You must give me the strength to live through this."

Glen and I clung to each other as we peered through the glass into that hospital nursery. I had only held Ethan twice and Glen had never been allowed to touch him. As Ethan's condition worsened, the nurse closed the drapes at the nursery window. We were separated completely from our little boy. A few minutes later Ethan joined his brother Jimmy in heaven.

I leaned my head heavily against Glen's shoulder as we drove silently home. The snow glistened in the moonlight, and I could hear the crunch of our tires against the half-frozen slush on the highway. My mind drifted back to that verse, "Go thy way; thy son liveth." What did it mean to me now?

Glen and I were preparing to move to California to join a Christian organization. We would be leaving our home, our family, and all our friends. I sensed God was saying through that verse, "Marilyn, continue with your plans; serve Me with all your heart, and don't worry about Ethan or Jimmy. They're both living with Me, and they're fine." I now believe that was what God was saying, but I couldn't receive that interpretation until later, when I had yielded my will to His.

I experienced many of the same adjustments after Ethan died as I did after Jimmy's death. We already had sent out birth announcements and an article had appeared in our local paper, so during the first few weeks after Ethan died, we often received congratulatory cards and sympathy cards in the same mail. I recall receiving two beautiful baby blue suits accompanied with a note, "Twins! I think you're one of the luckiest couples in the world!"

I didn't feel lucky; I felt plagued because our troubles were continuing. Shortly after Jimmy died I had begun to have a problem with recurring ovarian cysts which required several surgeries. Five weeks after Ethan died the pain began again. I had another cyst. We consulted several doctors who all recommended I have a total hysterectomy. After losing two babies in less than two years, the hope for more children was gone. While some of my friends were crying because of too many pregnancies, I was crying because I would never be pregnant again.

A month after that surgery, my grandmother died. As the family was preparing to leave the house for Grandma's funeral, Glen developed a migraine headache and went to bed. Then I began sobbing so violently someone had to give me a tranquilizer to calm me down enough that I could attend the funeral.

People couldn't understand why Glen and I were having such a difficult time with my grandmother's death. After all, she was in her seventies, she had lived a good life, and she didn't suffer long. No one took the time to consider what Glen and I had been through in the past year and a half. And the following year we moved four times, including the move from Indiana to California.

We moved from a large home into a tiny, two-bedroom apartment in San Bernardino, with rented furniture, and Matt and Mellyn were to sleep in bunk beds with Nate's crib in the same tiny room. The very first evening Glen had to work late so I began trying to get Matt and Mellyn settled into bed by myself. Just as they climbed in, the upper bunk came crashing down on top of Mellyn! Except for a few bumps and bruises, she was not injured, but the children all became hysterical. Overwhelmed and crying myself, I collapsed in the middle of the floor, and tried to comfort my three screaming children, all the while thinking, *And this is the great adventure God has called me to?*

When Nate was about eight months old, I went into a severe depression. I couldn't sleep; I cried a lot. And when I wasn't crying I was yelling at the children.

Glen was very patient with me, but he didn't know what was wrong. My Christian friends were certain it was a spiritual problem, and they kept asking, "Are you sure you understand the Spirit-filled life?"

My mother came to visit, took one look at me, and said, "This girl needs to go to bed." I had been running and running from my pain, but it finally had caught up with me.

No one had warned me that it was necessary to grieve, nor did anyone explain that, even though I had a baby and two other children to take care of, I would still miss Jimmy and Ethan. I was told that the adjustment to a hysterectomy was all in my head, and I was not informed about the changes that would occur in my body. Three babies, two funerals, four surgeries, and four moves in twenty-four months, and I was only twenty-eight. No wonder I was depressed!

My mother gave me the physical help I needed, the children matured, and I slowly grew accustomed to my grief. As the years went by I spent my time with my family, and God allowed the empty spots in my heart to be filled to some extent by other children, especially boys, who needed the attention I had time to give. We cooked for the band and bolstered the high school football team. Matt and Mellyn participated in various activities, and Glen, Nate, and I became their cheering section. Matt and Mellyn graduated and went on to college. In 1982, Mellyn married Mike Savage, a young man I had led to the Lord earlier.

That fall Nate began his junior year in high school. He had grown into a tall, handsome, sixteen-year-old young man. He was on the cross-country and basketball teams, sang in the ensemble, played trumpet in the pep band, and was on the honor roll.

Since I worked at the Christian high school where he attended, Nate and I spent a lot of time together driving to and from school. Although he was a very quiet boy, occasionally he shared something that gave me a hint of what was going on in his mind.

One morning on the way to school, he said, "Mom, have you ever wondered what Ethan looks like?"

I said, "Well, honey, you were identical twins; he must look just like you."

There was quiet for a moment, and then Nate said wistfully, "Boy, I sure would like to see him."

I chuckled rather uneasily, trying hard to cover up the strange feeling that flooded over me and replied, "Well, when we get to heaven, we'll all get to see him, and Jimmy, too."

The Rose of Sorrow

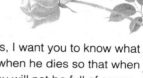

And now, dear brothers, I want you to know what
happens to a Christian when he dies so that when
it happens, you will not be full of sorrow,
as those are who have no hope.

1 THESSALONIANS 4:13, TLB

*O*n February 10, 1983, as we arrived at school, Nate scurried off with his friends to leave for a field trip. The day before I had heard him ask his brother, Matt, "Hey brother, how would you like to take a day off work?" Nate explained that his class was going to Los Angeles and they needed more cars and drivers. I wasn't surprised when Matt agreed to drive. He always was a softy when it came to his little brother.

Nate hardly had time to talk with me between his return from the field trip and leaving for the evening's basketball game. In fact, he was trotting backwards down the hall when I asked him what time he would be home.

"Oh, I don't know. The game might run kinda late, and it will take a while for the drive home. I'll call you if we're going to be really late."

He gave a quick wave and called, "Don't worry, Mom, I'll see ya later," as he dashed to his locker to get his uniform and gym bag.

That night my husband, Glen, went to his college class, and I spent a quiet evening alone. My mom called from San Diego where she and Dad were camping with some friends, and Mellyn called to check on details of the homecoming game the next evening at Nate's school. As I tried to watch television, I kept falling asleep, so I finally went to bed and slept soundly.

Suddenly, I awoke.

Where was I?

Why wasn't Glen in bed with me?

My thoughts were all jumbled. What time was it? My sleep-blurred eyes eventually focused on the clock. 11:44. I hurried down the hall to find Glen.

"Isn't Nate home yet?"

Glen shook his head.

With much uneasiness, I said, "Something must be wrong. He always calls if he's going to be late."

I tried to appear calm for Glen, but on the inside, I was crying, *Please bring him home, Lord; please bring him home.*

At first we hesitated to call anyone. *Surely it is just car trouble. He'll call us soon,* we reasoned. This was a new experience for us. Nate was always good about calling. My pride made it difficult for me to call others and admit I didn't know where my son was. But as it grew later and later, alarm overruled pride.

After several calls to Nate's coaches, we tried calling a friend who always rode with Nate. The sick feeling in my stomach grew when there was no answer at his house.

I thought, *His family never stays out late; they must have heard something. Why haven't we?*

Glen called another of Nate's friends, but her mom answered. Soon I heard Glen say, "What hospital are they in?"

As Glen was dialing the hospital, he said, "There's been a terrible head-on collision. All of the kids who were in Nate's car are in the hospital." The emergency room attendant told Glen they had a young male, listed as John Doe. I heard Glen say, "Does that mean he's dead?"

"He's alive but he's unconscious and unable to identify himself." The attendant continued, "Mr. Heavilin, come quickly."

I knocked on Matt's bedroom door, "Honey, there's been a bad accident. Get dressed quickly; we must hurry!"

Matt recalls:

"Mom didn't say who was in the accident. Grandma and Grandpa Willett were out of town that night—it could have been them. But I knew it was Nate. As I was numbly getting dressed, I thought, *We're going through another funeral.*

At twenty-four Matt was already well acquainted with grief.

It seemed I was moving in slow motion. I desperately needed to get to Nate and kept telling myself everything would be all right once we got there. I knew if I could touch him and speak to him, he would wake up. In my mind, I was talking to Nate all the while I was dressing. *Hang on, Nate. I'm coming; I'm coming. Just hang on.*

Our minds were in a fog, but we were functioning automatically in an organized manner. Matt remembered to take rolls of coins for phone calls, and I grabbed my address book, thinking, *We've got to call everybody and tell them to pray.* Then I thought of Glen's and my parents. How could we tell them Nate might be dying? Grandchildren aren't supposed to die.

It was the middle of the night and everything seemed so still. We passed the parents of one of the girls who'd been in Nate's car, heading to another hospital. We rolled down the car windows to exchange information.

"How's your daughter?" we asked.

"She's conscious and has many facial injuries. How's Nate?"

"He's unconscious—listed as a John Doe. Pray!"

As Glen drove, I prayed. The first of my prayer was simply, "God, is it happening again? We've already lost two children. Do we have to bear that pain again?"

At the hospital we hurried to the reception desk. "Where's Nate? How is he? Can we see him?" So many questions and no answers.

The nurse just said, "Someone will be out to see you shortly; please fill out these forms."

We struggled to focus our minds on car license numbers and insurance information. Finally Glen talked with a police officer who verified the car involved in the crash was ours, but told us nothing about Nate. He said the accident occurred at 11:44, the exact time I had awakened so suddenly! How thankful I am God awakened me so we were able to get to the hospital before it was too late, while Nate was still alive.

A security guard appeared, saying, "Clear the halls. We're bringing a patient through." We stood in a doorway to watch.

Several people huddled over the person on the cart, but I could see a head of tousled brown hair, a pair of blue jeans, and a big foot wearing a white sock. Just as the cart was pushed out of sight, I realized it was Nate. I wanted to run after him, but instead I just stood there numbly, trying to take in what I had seen.

My son, my Nate, lying on that cart, so helpless; my son who had looked anything but helpless as he grabbed his uniform and left for a physically taxing evening of basketball. "Oh God, please help him; please help us," I whispered.

Soon a nurse called us into a small, cluttered office, and in a warm, but very concerned voice, she said, "We have just taken your son to surgery. His leg has been crushed; he has brain damage and extensive damage to his heart and lungs. His heart stopped once already, and we opened his chest to massage the heart and start it again."

I felt sick as I envisioned someone's hands on my son's heart. My thoughts drifted back to the prayer I had prayed on the way to the hospital.

Lord, please don't let it be Nate's fault. Please heal all of the kids if it's Your will. Lord... I hesitated and began again, *Lord, we want Your will in Nate's life, and Lord, we're giving You power of attorney over Nate.*

As the nurse continued, I began to sense what God's will was for Nate. I asked the nurse, "Do you think he's going to make it?"

Her eyes dropped, and she shook her head, "No."

A kind-looking woman came up to me and said, "My brother was the driver of the other car. I'm so sorry. I'm so sorry. Is your son going to be all right?"

I answered very matter-of-factly, "My son is dying."

As she began to weep, I instinctively wrapped my arms around her ample frame and said, "It's OK. If Nate dies, I know he'll go to heaven and I'll see him again someday."

The lady stiffened a little and walked away. Perhaps my comments seemed too unfeeling, too calloused. They weren't meant to be. I realize now I was in the numbness of grief. God was speaking for me.

As Mellyn and Mike arrived, we hugged each other tightly, prayed, and waited. Eventually we learned that the three other students in Nate's car were seriously injured, but the doctors said they would survive. A prayer answered.

We also had learned the man who hit Nate had been arrested for drunk driving. I experienced anger and relief at the same time. It wasn't Nate's fault, another prayer answered, but my son was dying because someone had been foolish enough to drink and drive. My son, who never drank and who was from a family who didn't drink, was the victim of a drunk driver. How unfair!

The words "drunk driver" were still spinning in my mind as the nurse reentered the waiting room. When I saw her face, I knew.

"Is he gone?"

As she handed me a brown paper bag with his Nikes in it, she nodded, "Yes."

Glen came from around the corner, and I said, "Honey, he's gone." The hope left his eyes as he hugged me tightly and we wept.

Twenty-three years have passed since that agonizing evening, years filled with a mélange of emotions and questions. Why our son? Why did he have to die? Will the sick feeling in my stomach ever go away? Why didn't we at least have time to say goodbye?

I have felt anger at a justice system that didn't protect us from such happenings; jealousy toward others whose lives seemed to go untouched; resentment that it was my son instead of someone else's.

However, as I walked into Nate's memorial service and saw nearly a thousand people in attendance, I realized that God had allowed Nate to touch more lives in seventeen years than many of us touch in seventy; many of them young lives, people who still can have years of service for God.

Even now as I reread the numerous newspaper articles, including one with the headline: "Nathan lives now in his heavenly, not Heavilin home," I feel confident that Nate, in his life and in his death, was a witness to the entire community for his Lord Jesus.

His death also caused some adults to change their priorities. After Nate died, a coworker of Glen's began attending his own son's track meets regularly—time with his son became very precious.

A few weeks later a college representative was in my office and I shared my story with her. She asked, "Considering what you've just been through, do you have any specific advice for other parents?"

I responded, "Spend all of the time you can with your family. Always keep them on the top of your priority list." The next day she wrote me a letter.

"I want you to know that as a result of my conversation with you on Wednesday, I've canceled all my appointments for today and I'm going home to my son—first to attend his baseball game, then home to be with him."

I quickly saw God allow us to begin to influence lives around us because of our experience.

One month after Nathan's death, some of my students and I visited Biola University. As we rested in our dorm room we talked about what it was going to be like living without Nate. They commented:

"It's no fun at school anymore."

"I don't like to watch the basketball games now."

Then someone asked, "How can we ever enjoy Christmas again since Nate's birthday is Christmas Day?"

I muttered, "I'd like to ask God to cancel December because I don't want any part of Christmas." The thought of gifts, Christmas carols, and Christmas programs seemed incongruous with what we were facing.

The next morning the students visited some of the university classes, and my friend Diana and I wandered around the campus, ending up at the bookstore. I was aimlessly leafing through the display of posters when one caught my eye. I couldn't believe it. Through my tears, I called to Diana, "Come and look at this!"

The poster was of a beautiful red rose. The flower had opened and dewdrops were visible on the petals. At the bottom was a quote which conveyed a message from God to me that day.

It read, "GOD GIVES US MEMORIES SO WE MIGHT HAVE ROSES IN DECEMBER."[1]

My first thought was, *God, You've got to be kidding. Even in California we don't find many roses in December, and there certainly aren't any roses in my life right now.*

But I bought the poster, had it framed, and hung it in my bedroom. I glanced at it frequently and seemed to hear God say, "Marilyn, I'm not going to cancel December, but I've given you many, many wonderful memories of Nate. Gather and savor them because through those memories and through the special things I'm going to do for you this year and every year, you're going to have bouquets of roses, even in December. Keep looking for the roses!"

God continues to keep His promise by providing roses, sometimes with actual flowers, sometimes through friends, and often in the form of memories as a reminder He is caring for me, and when I hurt, He hurts.

A few months later I was helping a student with a scholarship notebook she had compiled. It included certificates showing her accomplishments, and pictures from high school yearbooks. I turned to a page with a group picture, and I didn't see anything else, only that Nate was in the picture. When I saw it, I was overwhelmed with sorrow and began to cry.

At that moment, Sally, the school secretary came into my office unaware of what had just happened. She was holding a rose.

She explained, "I bought this rose for someone else, but she isn't here today, and God just told me I should bring it to you!"

In the years since Nate's death, hardly a moment has gone by without me thinking of him. Knowing that God cares doesn't take the hurt away, but it does make the hurt bearable.

We have gathered many memories, each a beautiful rose.

One of my young friends, Darcy, gave me a notepad which states, "A rose is God's autograph." As I stroll in my rose garden of memories, I see God's autograph everywhere. Each rose is a special, signed gift from God reminding me of His care. And when the hurts become more than I can bear, it seems He always sends me another rose—a beautiful memory or a precious friend.

God continues to increase my bouquet of roses. Some have come with thorns, but God has helped me deal even with the thorns.

Perhaps you are going through a December in your life; a death, a divorce, or some other severe disappointment, and you can't see any roses. Let me share my December roses with you so you can start collecting a bouquet of your own and then share your roses with others.

The Rose of Comfort

Rejoice with them that do rejoice,
and weep with them that weep.

ROMANS 12:15

*W*hen we left the hospital after Nathan's death, the many friends who were waiting for us wanted to know, "What can we do for you?"

My response was, "Come home with us," because we did not want to walk into our house alone. We arrived at our home after 3 AM, and within an hour more than forty people were with us sitting in our living room having a prayer meeting.

Their friendship, even in the middle of the night, comforted me immeasurably. As we prayed, I sensed we were not the only ones who were grieving—we were not the only ones who would miss Nathan.

I will always remember my friend Donna Lynn's prayer because she thanked God for the memories and asked Him to help us concentrate on the good times. Her prayer came from the heart of one mother and touched the heart of another. At that moment, all I could remember were the times I had been upset with Nate and had made wrong decisions, but Donna Lynn's prayer helped me focus on the good times. I began to see that even though there were a few times I would like to have changed, the good memories far outweighed the not-so-good ones. Her positive prayer was a vital encouragement and comfort.

Early that morning, Vonette Bright, the wife of Dr. Bill Bright, the founder of Campus Crusade for Christ, arrived. After speaking at a prayer breakfast where she had shared about our tragedy, she came directly to our home.

Following her message, a young couple had come to her and said, "Vonette, we have a verse we would like you to take to your friend." When Vonette arrived at our home, she was excited even though she was broken for us. I must admit when she first said she had a verse she wanted to share with us, I thought *Dear Lord, please don't let it be Romans 8:28,* "And we know that all things work together for good to them that love God." I believe that verse, but just a few hours after my son's death, I could not fathom how any good could come out of the death of a seventeen-year-old.

But Vonette surprised me. She didn't give me Romans 8:28; she gave me a verse I had not noticed before. The verse reads: "The good men perish; the godly die before their time.... No one seems to realize that God is taking them away from evil days ahead. For the godly who die shall rest in peace" (Isaiah 57:1-2, TLB).

Five people shared that same verse with us by noon that day, so I knew God was trying to get a message across to me. Later I discovered J. Vernon McGee had preached from that text that morning on the radio. Since his program is broadcast at 7:30 AM in this area, many of our friends had been listening to him when they received the news about Nathan. What timing!

Through this verse, while I knew Nate was a good man, and seventeen was surely before his time, I also felt God was saying to me, "Marilyn, it wasn't an accident. I wasn't on vacation the night Nate died. I knew about it before it happened. Marilyn, I'm taking him away from something worse. He's with Me, and he's doing fine."

Over the years I've observed that, for the Christian, there are many things worse than death. I may not know until eternity all that God spared Nathan, but I can rest assured from now until then that Nate is with the Lord, and he is doing fine. I am so thankful Vonette took the time to visit me. My whole outlook might have been different if I hadn't received her comforting words that particular morning.

However, not all the words we received were comforting. Have you ever, in your eagerness to be helpful, said something you realized afterward could cause problems? One well-meaning lady heard my story and suggested we have someone pray over us to cleanse our blood lines! Another listener suggested our family was bound by a curse of death. After the death of each of my children at least one person recommended we confess the sin in our lives and another suggested that we needed more faith. I have begun to understand that most of these comments are motivated out of fear that the same thing could happen to them. If a person can come up with a reason for your trauma, they can believe that, if they avoid that particular pitfall, they will escape a similar experience.

While we were waiting at the hospital, I received a phone call from an acquaintance asking how Nate was doing. By then God had confirmed in my heart that Nate wasn't going to live, so I simply said, "Nate is dying." I expected her response to be similar to ours, feeling hurt, crushed, and disappointed.

Her response was different. She exclaimed, "Oh no, you can't give up. Death comes from Satan. If you give up, you're giving in to Satan, and if Nate dies, it will be because you gave up."

As I hung up the phone, I saw the nurse coming to tell us Nate was dead. The words rang in my ears, "Nate died because you gave up."

As we walked out of the hospital into the parking lot, I asked God to give me a verse which would comfort me. Part of one verse, "Precious in the sight of the LORD is the death of His saints" (Psalm 116:15), and another, "Thine eyes have seen my unformed substance; And in Thy book they were all written, the days that were ordained for me, when as yet there was not one of them" (Psalm 139:16, NASB), came to me immediately.

Later, however, the woman's words came back to haunt me again and again. Glen helped me resolve the matter when he said, "Marilyn, you never gave up on Nate, but you gave him OVER to God."

Glen was right. He reminded me of the prayer I had prayed on the way to the hospital. "God, we give You power of attorney in Nathan's life. We trust he is going to be fine, but if that isn't Your will, it's OK. We are turning the controls over to You."

Whenever I saw this lady after Nate's death, I had to remind myself, "I didn't give up; I gave over." In my heart, I was sure I hadn't given up on Nate, but I knew she still thought I had. I wanted to cry every time I saw her. Her words put a wall between us which would not be torn down easily nor soon.

"It is harder to win back the friendship of an offended brother than to capture a fortified city. His anger shuts you out like iron bars" (Proverbs 18:19, TLB).

For those who want to comfort others, I would caution you to be sensitive. When you are talking with those who are going through trauma, allow for the work that God is doing in their hearts, and take your cue from what they say.

In our case, God was very clearly preparing us for Nathan's death even as we drove to the hospital. He was working with us and planting peace in our hearts. Those who were close to us sensed it immediately. Nate didn't die because we had "given up"; Nate died because God said, "I miss you, Nate; come on home."

It is very important to acknowledge a person's loss quickly, through a note, a card, or a personal visit, but don't feel you must explain or justify the trauma.

Of all the ways you can help those in crisis, offering "words of wisdom" can be the most risky. Even if your suggestions or philosophy are positive, they may not be accepted in a positive manner by those who are in the middle of the trauma.

Dr. Henry Brandt has been my personal friend for over fifty years, and we have been through many trials together. I trust him and often ask for his counsel. Uncle Henry, as I fondly call him, spent the weekend with us after Nate's death. I was glad he came.

Each time I began to get upset because of the circumstances we were facing, Uncle Henry would lovingly put his arm around me, hug me, and say, "And let the peace of God rule in your hearts" (Colossians 3:15).

His words were scriptural—but each time he hugged me and made me the benefactor of his spiritual insight, I got angry.

I knew what he was trying to say. He was pointing out that my peace should come from Christ and not from my circumstances, but I didn't want to hear it. My son was dead; why should I want peace?

Fortunately, Dr. Brandt and I knew each other well enough so that he could risk my anger. As my anger dwindled, through Uncle Henry's words I was able once again to ask God for His peace so that I could face this December of my life victoriously.

My rule of thumb when talking to a bereaved person is: If you don't know what to say, if you aren't sure how God is working in the situation, just hug the person. Offer advice only sparingly.

If you are the one who is suffering, and if people have said things which seem insensitive or do not help or comfort when you are grieving, ask God to guide your response. It is unlikely they meant to be unkind; in fact, as in Dr. Brandt's case, they may be saying what you need to hear. Try to learn from the experience and be sensitive and compassionate as you deal with others.

Before you try to console with words, make sure you have already established a good rapport with the bereaved, and don't be offended if your advice is not immediately accepted. I'm glad Dr. Brandt was willing to take the risk, and I'm also thankful he stuck with me even when I didn't want to accept his advice.

As comforters, we should tread softly. Sometimes there isn't anything we can say except, "I love you; I'm praying for you, and I'm here for you."

"From a wise mind comes careful and persuasive speech" (Proverbs 16:23, TLB).

Let me suggest some other forms of encouragement and comfort you can offer which may minimize your risk of saying the wrong thing.

In spite of sorrow, people still need to eat, but few bereaved people have the motivation or strength to prepare meals for themselves. If you like to cook and have the time, your favorite dish will be much appreciated by a grieving family. I found it helpful when friends brought food that had been packaged in freezable containers, so that we could enjoy their contributions weeks later.

You don't have to be a gourmet cook to help. Shortly after breakfast on that fateful Friday morning, my friend Jackie arrived with a sack of groceries: cheese, crackers, bread, cinnamon rolls, other snacks, napkins, and paper plates. This helped tremendously.

Several years ago the teenage son of a man who served on a church board with Glen died very suddenly. I felt we should visit the family right away, but since we didn't know them well, I was a little nervous.

I took a loaf of homemade bread out of my freezer, thinking, *Even if they don't want to see us, they'll like my bread*. We went to their door armed with my bread. A friend of the family welcomed us, accepted the bread, and invited us in.

We found the family and their close friends so dazed by the circumstances surrounding the boy's death that no one seemed able to think about what needed to be done. I asked, "Has the pastor been called?"

"No."

"Have friends been called?"

"No."

No plans had been made for meals or for accommodations for relatives who would be coming from out of town.

When I asked if I could stay and help with some of those details, they readily accepted.

Glen returned home to take care of our children, and I stayed until late that evening. I returned daily for the next several days to help with funeral arrangements, make phone calls, and plan meals, and the mother even asked me to help her clean out their son's room. A simple loaf of bread had opened the door and made it possible for me to see the needs and to help the family in a very vital way.

One act of kindness I particularly appreciated was when people brought pictures of Nathan which they had taken. Some were of events we had also photographed but were different poses or groupings. Others laminated newspaper articles of the accident and funeral for us.

Several of Nathan's classmates cleaned our house the week after Nate's death. Two of them, Debbie and Julie, offered to come on a weekly basis for the remainder of the school year. What a blessing!

I am an organized person and under normal circumstances have no trouble keeping my house clean, but during this time, cleaning a bathroom or running a vacuum were of little importance to me. I used all of the strength I had just to function at work. When I got home I collapsed into a chair. I didn't have the emotional or physical strength to do much cleaning or cooking. I am so grateful these girls saw my need and were willing to commit themselves to help.

God also had a special bonus in store for all of us through this. Two years later Debbie became my daughter-in-law! We both look back to her "housecleaning days" as a wonderful time for a future mother-in-law and daughter-in-law to get to know each other. Debbie is one of our very beautiful and special roses.

We received more than six hundred cards and letters after Nathan's death, and they still comfort me. The cards with personal notes were especially meaningful.

Many people chose to telephone us rather than to come to the house. This was fine, but often I could not talk long because of all the activity in our home, and I was sorry I couldn't reach out and hug those people.

Some people sent telegrams of condolences, and we appreciated their thoughtfulness. We also appreciated the flowers and plants which were sent to the house. They were lovely reminders of those who grieved with us.

There are a number of details connected with funeral arrangements which will need to be taken care of, and I have put together a checklist which I hope will be helpful. Many of these things can be done by a close friend or family member.

_____ Call the pastor

_____ Call relatives

_____ Call family attorney

_____ Locate any existing will

_____ Call insurance companies

_____ Locate all insurance policies and bank accounts

_____ Check on existing retirement funds

_____ Notify Social Security

_____ Help write obituary

_____ Help plan funeral

_____ Go with bereaved to mortuary and cemetery

_____ Provide guest book to use at bereaved's home

_____ Find someone to provide family meals

_____ Clean the house

_____ Mow the lawn

_____ Grocery shop (especially for munchies and finger foods, paper products: tissues, toilet tissue, towels, plates, cups, napkins, etc.)

_____ Do minor house and car repairs

_____ Have someone stay at house during funeral

_____ Have someone record food and flowers brought to the home

The evening after the accident was our school's first homecoming event. Nate and the other boy injured in the accident both played trumpet in the pep band. How can a pep band be peppy without trumpets? Helen, a mother of students at the school, and an accomplished trumpet player, asked herself that question and came up with a solution.

She stopped by our house and said, "If you'll give me Nate's music, I would like to play the trumpet for him tonight at Homecoming if it's OK with you." Helen found a unique way to help in our time of need.

Shortly after Nathan's death I attended the funeral of another young man, a father, also killed by a drunk driver. Someone had put together a photo album of pictures portraying the man's life. In addition, a collage of pictures was displayed on an easel—beautiful memories for us all to enjoy. What a special tribute.

This man left a young son who had very little time to collect memories of his daddy. As we entered the viewing room at the funeral home, a nicely printed note was placed on a table along with blank pages of paper. The note asked us to write about a memory we had of the deceased. These were to be placed in a notebook to be given to his son when he became old enough to appreciate it. That notebook will, for many years, give the son a much-needed link to the father he never knew.

After my friend Barbara's house burned in a Southern California fire, she recalled:

"One friend went through her entire house and boxed up a wide assortment of things that she felt she would need if she had nothing. She brought items from shampoo and bobby pins to towels and face cloths and even flannel pajamas for my husband.

"At Christmas one young man brought an umbrella, jigsaw puzzles for our family, and tools for my husband.

"One dear lady who is extremely shy came by with some lovely clothes (some brand new) in the exact size I needed, and when she was gone we discovered rolls and a pie and all sorts of other special things. I'm not sure she ever said a word, but we will never forget what her actions said."

When another friend and her children were trying to recover from an unexpected and unwanted divorce, she greatly appreciated the families who invited her children on outings with them. She also recalls how often she wished for someone to do needed repairs around the house or simple maintenance work on the car.

I have one I-wish-we-would-have-done-that suggestion. It would have been helpful later if we had had a guest book at our home to record the names of friends who came or brought in food. Several hundred people came through our home that week, and I wish I had a way of remembering all of them.

I also wish someone could have helped us think in those hours just after Nate's death. Glen and I both regret we weren't able to donate some of Nate's organs to a needy person, and we are sorry we didn't ask to see Nate at the hospital after he died. Now we realize that neither of us had been convinced absolutely that it was really Nate until we saw his body in the casket. We had both wanted to see him at the hospital, but weren't able to verbalize our thoughts.

When you are with the bereaved, be a good listener. Encourage them to express themselves freely. Don't reprove them for what they say or feel, but help them voice their feelings and try to understand them. We often tend to stay away when friends hurt because we can think of no specific way to help. I discovered, after Nathan's death, that the little things meant as much as the big things. Even when we are in the midst of grief ourselves, we can be a rose to others around us who are hurting if we are willing to be sensitive to their needs.

The Rose of Forgiveness

Let all bitterness, and wrath, and anger,
and clamour, and evil speaking, be put
away from you, with all malice: And be ye
kind one to another, tenderhearted,
forgiving one another, even as God for
Christ's sake hath forgiven you.

EPHESIANS 4:31-32

*H*ave you forgiven him yet?"

"How do you feel about him?"

These were the questions people asked the first days after our son was killed by a drunk driver. At the time, the easiest thing to say was, "I don't know how I feel about him." I was trying to cope with Nate's death. I couldn't deal with the driver right then.

That answer got me through the first few weeks, but then I started asking myself the same questions.

"How do I feel about him? Have I forgiven him?"

I was afraid to meet him face-to-face because I didn't know how I felt. What would I do when I had to see the man who killed my son, the man who had robbed us of the privilege of watching Nate grow up?

When I learned the accident had been caused by a drunk driver, anger had overwhelmed me, but then I remembered I had experienced those same feelings of anger when Ethan died. At that time my anger wasn't directed toward a drunk driver— my anger was directed toward God. I felt I had been "done in" by God. I had trusted Him and told Him He could have His will in Ethan's life. Instead of healing Ethan, He had let him die.

My anger began to simmer into bitterness until I read a statement from Dr. S.I. McMillen's book, *None of These Diseases*.

> The moment I start hating a man, I become his slave. I can't work any more because he even controls my thoughts. My resentments produce too many stress hormones in my body and I become fatigued after only a few hours of work. The work I formerly enjoyed is now drudgery....
>
> The man I hate hounds me wherever I go. I can't escape his tyrannical grasp on my mind.[1]

My anger and hatred hadn't been focused on a person, but on a situation. I was angry because Ethan was dead, and that anger was controlling me. After reading Dr. McMillen's words, I was able to confess my anger as sin and ask the Lord to help me be content in my situation.

When I learned Nathan had been killed by a drunk driver, those same feelings of anger and hatred welled up within me. I didn't want to be a slave to anger again, so I immediately asked God to remove those feelings and give me victory in the midst of this terrible situation. However, my prayer was not put to the test until the time I met the man who was responsible, face-to-face.

As I entered the second-floor hallway the first day we were to appear in court, I saw a man sitting in a wheelchair. I just knew he must be the one. As I walked closer to the wheelchair, it turned, and I saw the man's face. He looked like a very frightened man—not a killer at all.

I didn't feel angry, nor did I want to scream or lash out at him—I just stood and let the tears fall. God had removed the bitterness and was allowing me to forgive this man.

Besides forgiveness, I also felt relief when I saw the man's face—relief that I was Nate's mother rather than this man's mother.

I sensed that this man's sin had caused his family deep heartache, and I was relieved that Nate had never brought us heartache, shame, or grief during all his seventeen years. We weren't having to help our child work through the guilt he would experience at causing someone else's death.

In the magazine *Family Life Today,* Lewis Smedes identifies four stages of forgiving.

> The first stage is hurt: When somebody causes you pain so deep and unfair that you cannot forget it, you are pushed into the first stage of the crisis of forgiving.
>
> The second stage is hate: You cannot shake the memory of how much you were hurt, and you cannot wish your enemy well. You sometimes want the person who hurt you to suffer as you are suffering.
>
> The third stage is healing: You are given eyes to see the person who hurt you in a new light. Your memory is healed, you turn back the flow of pain and are free again.
>
> The fourth stage is the coming together: You invite the person who hurt you back into your life; if he or she comes honestly, love can move you both toward a new and healed relationship. The fourth stage depends on the person you forgive as much as it depends on you; sometimes he doesn't come back and you have to be healed alone.[2]

Nate died in February, but I didn't see the driver of the other car until several months later. God needed that time to prepare my heart and get me ready to be forgiving.

I went through all of the stages Dr. Smedes mentioned. The hurt I felt seemed unbearable. Nate was gone. I would never see him on this earth again, and I was completely broken. A total stranger had caused us this relentless, throbbing pain.

Although I didn't actually hate the man, I hated the fact he could thoroughly disrupt our lives and throw us into such chaos, and still walk around free, seemingly unscathed.

The summer after Nate's death, I was trying to locate a friend's home, and I got lost. I looked up at the street sign and realized I was on the street where the man lived who had killed Nate. I didn't want to be there, but before I could find a place to turn around, I saw him. His wheelchair was off to the side on the lawn—he had recovered enough from the accident to be out of it for a while. He was on his feet, playing ball with his son.

After I turned the corner, I parked the car and cried. I hated it that he—the man who killed my son—could enjoy a summer afternoon with his son. He robbed me of a privilege he was still experiencing. Oh, how I wished he could feel my devastation and my sorrow.

The beginning of healing came when I met him in the courtroom because I was able to see him in a new light, not only as the man who had come crashing into our lives, who had seemed to have little regard for our feelings, but I was able to see him also as a frightened, needy man.

Because of the legal circumstances there has been no "coming together." I have experienced my healing alone. Although I have never been able to share my feelings with the man who caused Nate's death, God has healed me enough so that I am able to pray that God will bring him peace.

As Christians, we mistakenly expect all victims to be ready to offer instant forgiveness to those who have hurt them. A friend came to me the morning after Nathan died and asked me to go to the hospital to tell the driver of the other car I had forgiven him. In the middle of the night Glen and I had called the hospital chaplain, who is a friend of ours, and asked him to see the man as soon as possible, but I was not ready to meet him face-to-face.

Another acquaintance was so insistent I display forgiveness immediately, she sent a card to the man, signing our family's name along with hers, stating, "We love you and forgive you."

I could have gone to the hospital immediately, or quickly sent a card proclaiming forgiveness, but in my case it would have been premature. At that point, I couldn't even understand what all I needed to forgive him of; I hadn't lived long without Nate. For me, forgiving has come in segments. Each time I hold a new grandchild, each time I attend the wedding of one of Nate's friends, each time I attend a family reunion...each time, I can forgive just a little bit more.

When we are grieving, we shouldn't feel compelled to rush forgiveness. It may be necessary to allow time for the situation to sink in and for God to do a work in our hearts. If you are the one who is grieving, be open to God's guiding and allow Him to lead you in the direction of forgiveness. I am not condoning vengeance or uncontrolled anger, but you may find there is a neutral stage where you have no feelings one way or the other; you are numb. The neutral stage can be a provision from God to protect you from feelings of grief or anger which would be too great for you to control. Forgiveness, especially in a traumatic or crisis situation, will take time. Give God time. Give yourself time.

Although God helped me control the feelings of bitterness and anger toward the drunk driver, I allowed myself to get tripped up in another area.

Because all of the teenagers in Nathan's car came from Christian families, I hoped we would be able to work together in harmony. However, we had difficulty agreeing about anything. Consequently, the insurance settlement, which we had hoped would happen in sixty to ninety days, took fifteen months—months of problems and hurt feelings. And my bitterness grew.

I knew God could help me overcome these feelings, but I didn't want His help. I preferred to sit and stew. Why couldn't the other families understand we needed to get all of the legal matters behind us? It was as though we were waiting for the benediction at the funeral. We couldn't make decisions on our own, and we couldn't control our schedule. Every time I thought I was beginning to learn to handle things, we would get a call from an attorney or the insurance company, and it would start all over again. I was angry at the situation and at the people who were "allowing everything to drag on so long."

When I saw the other families, my hands shook; when they called, I cried. I was allowing my anger to dictate my reactions to everything and everyone around me.

One day when the anger was boiling especially hot inside of me, I received a note from a friend. It said, "Marilyn, I don't understand everything that you're going through, but I have one thought I would like to share with you. 'Keep the wound clean.'"

What timing! My first reaction was to throw that card across the room and yell, "What does she know about my pain?" But then my heart began to soften and I burst into tears as I cried out to God for help. I had not kept the wound clean but had allowed it to fester with so much bitterness. As I confessed my sin to the Lord, I asked Him to forgive me and help me cleanse the wound of anything which would keep it from healing properly: the anger, the bitterness, the frustration, the impatience. The desire for these attitudes to leave came immediately, but it took, and still takes, lots of work and determination to keep the festering from beginning again. I have spent much time in study and prayer, asking God to help me "keep the wound clean."

Joni Eareckson Tada's book *A Step Further* helped me to look at our situation from others' points of view and to learn to forgive others. Joni explains:

> It's a kind of scale, I finally reasoned. Every person alive fits somewhere onto a scale of suffering that ranges from little to much.
>
> And it's true. Wherever we happen to be on that scale—that is, however much suffering we have to endure—there are always those below us who suffer less, and those above who suffer more. The problem is we usually like to compare ourselves only with those who suffer less. That way we can pity ourselves and pretend we're at the top of the scale. But when we face

reality and stand beside those who suffer more, our purple-heart medals don't shine so brightly.[3]

God let me see I had become pious about my suffering. After all, how many people do you know who have buried three children? I placed myself rather high on the scale of suffering; surely no one had suffered more than I had.

God rebuked me for my attitude and showed me many people who have suffered more. At first I resisted the idea, but I finally had to admit I didn't know what it was like to be a Joni Eareckson, confined to a wheelchair for the rest of my life, or to suffer through a divorce, or sit by the bed of a child who was in a coma. Many people were experiencing griefs at least equal to if not greater than mine.

I had to ask God to forgive me for my self-righteous attitudes and to help me show compassion toward those who are suffering, whether or not their problems seem of great significance to me.

As I did this, God began to give me a greater compassion toward those with whom I had been angry. Perhaps they were experiencing the same thing I had experienced. From their position on the scale of suffering, they also might be having a hard time realizing that someone else could suffer more than they. I began to pray for them daily, that God would supply their needs, and give them peace and understanding. I prayed the same prayer for myself. A short time later, one of the families came to us and asked our forgiveness for their lack of understanding and compassion. God does hear and answer our prayers, but many times the work has to begin with us. As I asked God to remove the roots of bitterness, He answered my prayer and replaced those bitter roots with roots of love and compassion.

God is kind in that He doesn't dump all of our faults on us at once. He knows how much we can handle at one time. God gave me the desire to forgive the drunk driver; then, many months later, He gently showed me that my attitude toward the other families was wrong and I obediently confessed my sin.

Nearly three years after Nate's death, I participated in a communion service with a small group of people. The leader suggested we ask God to show us any sin in our lives regarding the other people in the room, then with family members, and finally with others with whom we associated. As I prayed, I felt no problem with anyone in the group nor with my family, but as my thoughts moved on to others, God stopped me short.

I could hear the voice of the lady who told me, "Nate is dying because you have given up." I tried to reason, "But Lord, she's the one who needs forgiving; I didn't do anything wrong." Instantly, God allowed me to see the bitterness that I had harbored against her. As I asked God to forgive me, a great load lifted from me, and then I was free to forgive my friend. God knew when I was able to deal with that sin, and He did not confront me with it until that time.

I have spoken on forgiveness many times and to hundreds of bereaved people through the years. As I have interacted with these hurting people, I have seen a pattern emerge. We tend to put those we need to forgive into several groups: the perpetrator, family and friends, ourselves, the person who died, and God.

The perpetrator can be the one who actually killed our loved one, or it may be someone who failed to do his job, such as a doctor or a caregiver. We also may need to forgive someone who failed to carry out justice. The man who killed our son was offered a plea bargain by the courts and was sentenced to three years probation, two hundred hours community service, and not a day in jail! I wasn't nearly as angry at the drunk driver as I was at the justice system. (I call it the "Injustice System.") One day as I was reading the Bible I came across Psalm 82. "God stands up to open heaven's court. He pronounces judgment on the judges. How long will you judges refuse to listen to the evidence? How long will you shower special favors on the wicked?...In death you are mere men. You will fall as any prince—for all must die" (Psalm 82:1-2,6-7, TLB).

I am chuckling as I write this because right beside those verses, I wrote *"You'll get yours!"* That was the day I was able to say, "God, the justice system isn't doing its job, and I'm really fed up with this. However, today I'm turning this whole system over to you. Go get 'em!" I haven't released the justice system from responsibility for wrong decisions; I've just turned them over to a Higher Court!

That does not mean I've given up trying to change the system. I am a faithful voter, and I write letters to people of influence when I'm concerned about a situation. I have a cell phone in my car so that I can report drunk drivers. But I'm not obsessed by these problems, and I have relinquished to God my desire for vengeance.

I define *forgiving* as giving up our claim to avenge a wrongdoing. When we forgive, we are not saying what the person did is acceptable; we are simply saying, I *am releasing myself from the responsibility of vengeance.* That process may not affect the one who hurt you at all, but it will set you free.

The bereaved often share with me how disappointed they are in their family and friends who seemed indifferent to their loss or said and did very hurtful things. I seldom recommend confrontation with someone who has hurt you because often the breech is made even larger when we try to confront. However, I highly recommend writing a letter to that person, stating exactly how you feel and what pain they have caused you. It may be helpful then to read that letter to a third party so that you feel you have been heard. Sometimes I place a chair in the middle of the room, imagine the person who has hurt me is sitting in that chair, and then I read my letter out loud. After you have voiced your hurt, I suggest you burn the letter or run it through a shredder. Create a little ceremony for yourself. Record your actions in your journal or some other safe place. "On this day, I forgave (the person's name), and I am relinquishing them and their actions to God."

After Nathan's death, I also had to forgive myself. Some of you may have to go through that too, especially if you were involved in the incident which caused your pain. "Why didn't I see it coming? Why didn't I know? Why didn't I sense it?"

I wasn't with Nathan the night he was killed, so I kept thinking, *Why didn't I go to that basketball game with him?* Though I wouldn't have been riding with him if I had gone, it was different from normal that I didn't go. So I reasoned that must be why it happened. I failed. I wasn't a good parent that night. I didn't go to the basketball game.

I was a great parent, and I knew it at the time. But for a while, I kept thinking, *Why didn't I pay more attention? If I had known...*I finally had to say, "Marilyn, if there's anything you've done wrong, I forgive you." I just had to look myself in the mirror and say, "I know you're a nice lady. I know you love Nathan. You did everything you could. If you made mistakes, I forgive you."

If you have a friend who is struggling with forgiving someone, don't condemn him for his feelings. The best thing you can do is to serve as a sounding board and pray him through the forgiving process.

A year or so after Nathan's death, I went through a day of prayer and emotional healing with a group called Philippian Ministries. I spent a morning talking through my life. Then in the afternoon the prayer director worked with me and we prayed through different situations. I talked with God about significant people in my life and asked forgiveness for wrong things I had done toward them. During this time the director asked if I could tell God that I forgave Nathan for dying.

I just about jumped out of my chair. I said, "It wasn't his fault!"

She said, "I know that, but can you forgive him for dying?"

"Well, of course, because it wasn't his fault!"

She said, "Fine. Why don't you say that to God?"

I tried to say it, but I couldn't get the words out. It took me a long time. I sat there and cried and prayed. Finally, the first words that came out were, "Nate, why'd you leave me so soon?" I realized I was mad at him. I know that's not logical, but I can guarantee some of you are also mad at an innocent party. You may be thinking, *Couldn't you have noticed the danger? Couldn't you sense you were in trouble? Couldn't you have done something different? Why didn't you take better care of yourself? You should have noticed that lump sooner. Why did you leave me in such a financial mess?*

Many times as I went down the freeway I would look at the exit Nate took the night of the accident, and I would think, *Nate, why didn't you take Waterman instead of Del Rosa? Couldn't you have done better? Couldn't you see that car coming? Why didn't you get there a little sooner or a little later?* All of those things may seem silly now, yet I needed to release my feelings and admit there was something that made me mad at Nate even though I loved him and would have given my life for him.

There also came a point when I needed to forgive God. God in Himself never needs forgiveness, but there are times in our lives when, from our point of view, things look so unfair, so hurtful, that we need to say, "God, I forgive You. I don't understand. From my vantage point, it seems You really hurt me. I know You have a purpose, and You have the road map, but I don't. I can't always see Your plan, and from my point of view, it doesn't make any sense." It is not sacrilegious to say, "God, I forgive You." It is an exercise we may need to go through to get back on speaking terms with God and acknowledge the severe pain we have gone through.

If you are hurting because someone has caused you a deep and unfair pain and you have been pushed into the "crisis stage" of forgiving, give yourself time. Give God time. Your responsibility is to make sure you don't allow the wound to fester with anger and bitterness. Keep the wound clean. Stay open with God. He will lead you into forgiveness.

As you offer the rose of forgiveness to someone else, you will receive your own rose, that great gift of freedom from the bondage of anger and bitterness.

The Rose of Remembrance

I thank my God upon every
remembrance of you.

PHILIPPIANS 1:3

*G*len and I sometimes attend The Compassionate Friends in Riverside. Each month, as newly bereaved parents come, they ask similar questions:

"Why don't people mention his name?"

"Why don't they talk about him?"

"Have they forgotten him already?"

Non-bereaved friends say, "We don't want to remind you of your loss or give you added grief, so it seems better not to talk about your child any more."

In Joe Bayly's book, *The Last Thing We Talk About,* Mr. Bayly writes that his little girl described her feelings about her brother's impending death as being "like something is pinned to the front of your mind all the time."[1]

Most people who have lost a loved one will agree with her. Everything else that goes into our mind has to be filtered through the thought, *My wife (or my husband or my child or my parent) is dead.* Rarely will you remind family members of something they are not already thinking about. You can be sure they will remember birthdays, the anniversaries of the death, and most assuredly the events which led up to the death.

One of my greatest dreads was the arrival of an anniversary of Nate's death when no one remembered. I realized my friends had been unusually faithful, but I knew there would undoubtedly come a time when I would not receive a card or a phone call on that very significant day. On the day of the eighth anniversary, I did not receive a card or a call from anyone who had known Nate although I did receive cards from some later in the week. But on the actual anniversary, none of their cards arrived. However, I did receive two cards from people who had read my books and were wanting to thank me for what my books had meant to them as well as acknowledging the anniversary of Nate's death. What a beautiful aroma those special roses brought into my life that day!

The week of Nate's crash I had been very busy working on student aid applications, along with a national scholarship application which was due that week. As a counselor, I did those things the same month of each year. For two or three years after the accident I still got very depressed when I started working on those applications. It was as if I were heading toward the crash again, and it helped when people acknowledged that that time of year must be hard for me.

Some people say, "I don't want to mention it because I may cause you more hurt." I am going to hurt whether they mention it or not because I can't get away from reminders; they are all around me. When friends mention the anniversary date is coming up, they are reminding me of the accident, but they're also reminding me they are hurting with me. They're supporting me, and they care for me.

Although friends may mean well, their avoidance of talking about the one who has died can hurt the bereaved family deeply. I talk about Nate often because I enjoy talking about him. Acknowledging his existence helps keep him alive in my mind, and it is important to me to remember the normal, natural, human things about him.

From my loss of Jimmy and Ethan, I realize memories do fade. I didn't have either of those babies long enough to have many memories. Now, years later, I can barely picture their faces. When Nate died, I began to fear that in a few years I wouldn't be able to remember him clearly, so I asked for a special gift from the Lord. I prayed I would always be able to see an image in my mind of Nate alive, and I would be able to remember the sound of his voice. God granted my request in a unique and special way.

Shortly after the accident we learned Nate's coach had video-taped a basketball game less than two weeks before Nate died. On that tape, Nate is real. He directs traffic as he dribbles the ball down the court and he puts his arm around the coach as the coach gives him some new piece of strategy. I can see him pat another player on the back as he enters the game, and he even makes six points. Whenever I watch the tape, I still find myself cheering for him when he makes a good play. My memory of Nate alive is preserved forever on that tape.

More than two and a half years after Nate's death, I started to play a cassette tape of myself which I had recorded when I was speaking at a luncheon a few months earlier. I inadvertently placed the tape into the recorder on the wrong side. I listened to the woman speaking and thought, *Who is that? That isn't my voice.*

As I listened, I heard a piano and a male voice. I quickly realized I had discovered a tape of one of Nathan's voice lessons! I prayed, "Oh God, please let me hear him clearly; don't tease me with this." Then I reasoned, *How can even God change something that happened over two years ago?* As Nate began to sing, the teacher said, "Nate, come up here by me," and she moved him right next to the tape recorder. I could hear him perfectly. I learned that day that the God I serve can answer prayers even retroactively!

I sat on the floor of our living room sobbing as I heard Nate sing one song and discuss it with his teacher. She asked, "Nate, do you have any more songs?"

He answered, "I've got one more. It isn't my favorite, but it's my mom's favorite and I want to learn it for her!"

I felt I had moved back in time, back to when things were normal, back when I couldn't comprehend how much emotional pain one body could stand. I hungrily devoured each precious note as Nate sang the beautiful Jewish-sounding melody, "Pierce My Ear, O Lord."

When Nate finished, the teacher said, "Nate, that was beautiful. I understand why your mom likes that song."

In his typical phlegmatic fashion, Nate said, "Yeah, not much melody, but kind of mellow."

Can you possibly imagine the joy I felt as I listened to my Nate sing? It was like a special delivery letter from heaven. More than two years after Nate's death, God answered my request that I would never forget the sound of his voice.

Most people want to talk about their deceased loved one, they hunger for even small reminders, and they want you, as their friends, to help them keep the memory of that person alive. One bereaved parent stated, "A person's not dead until he's forgotten."

Obviously, this is an area where you must be sensitive. Let the bereaved person set the pace. If he changes the subject when you mention the deceased's name, he may be trying to tell you that it hurts too much right now to talk about his loss. Just follow his lead.

Nate was a cross-country runner. The fall after he died, many of his close friends were on the cross-country team at school. Christian, one of Nate's best friends, asked me to come and watch them run. I enjoyed the meet, but, as the runners crossed the finish line, my mind flashed back to the previous year when Nate placed high enough to qualify for the league finals. A few tears slipped down my cheeks, but I wasn't embarrassed because I looked up and saw Christian's father had tears in his eyes also. He came over, put his arm around me, and said, "I'm thinking about him, too."

Many of Nate's friends wrote me notes with little stories about him. Sue, one of his classmates, wrote:

One of the things that I continue to be thankful for is the precious memories I have of Nate. I miss walking through the halls and singing with Nate. He always had a song that he would share. He often asked me how he could help when no one else knew I was down. He carried my burdens. He was and is a dear friend. I just wanted you to share my thankfulness.

I dreaded the approach of June of 1984 because Nate would have graduated then. At baccalaureate the students presented a slide show of Nathan which they had compiled, with a tape of B.J. Thomas singing "Home Where I Belong" as background music. After the program they presented the slides and tape to me with this note:

Dear Mrs. Heavilin,
   This slide show in no way expressed all that Nathan was to us or to you; but, in a way, the words of the song, "Home Where I Belong," expressed our security in the fact that we will see Nate again.
   We also pray that this little token of our love for Nate will continually remind you of our support for you and your family.
   Nathan was an irreplaceable part of our class; but Nathan is home where he belongs.
   With all our love in Him, the class of 1984.

As the school counselor, it was my job to present all of the scholarships and awards at the graduation ceremonies. I prayed God would dry up my seemingly never-ending well of tears as I prepared for that event the year Nate should have graduated from high school.

Each year the seniors give roses to their parents during the ceremony. As a faculty member, I handed the roses to the students so they could take them to their parents.

Many thoughts flooded my mind as I passed a flower to each student. *One of these should be mine. I wonder how Nate would give it to me. He would probably do something silly. He might be giggling.* Most of all, I was thinking, *I want a rose. I feel cheated and left out.*

After the students had returned to the platform, I saw two of the seniors walking toward me with a bouquet of roses and I was instantly overwhelmed! Their thoughtfulness assured me they cared for me and they missed Nate, too. God allowed me to see He was working in those teenagers' lives. He was making them more serious than most students would be on graduation night, and they were learning compassion through Nate's death.

Their action released both me and the audience to cry together. If I had fallen apart while making the scholarship presentations, I would have been crying alone in front of an audience of several hundred people. But the students' kind gesture made my loss public enough so that it was acceptable for us all to cry together. After a minute or so, we regained our composure and were able to proceed with the ceremony. Acknowledgment of my grief was very important to me because it gave me courage to go on.

For the next twelve years Glen and I attended the graduation and awarded a Nathan Heavilin Memorial Scholarship to one of the students. I watched with much emotion as the graduates went out into the audience to give their parents a rose. I was also able to watch with interest and anticipation because each year one of the graduates presented me with a rose. During those years, this quiet little tradition helped me know Nate was not forgotten, and I'm sure it also served as a reminder to each parent of how fortunate they were as their child brought a rose to them. And best of all, I got a very special hug from a teenager. How I cherished those hugs!

When others acknowledge that a situation might be hard, it often bolsters people to bravery. But when the bereaved are placed in a situation which is going to be difficult, and everyone goes on as if nothing has happened, it is much harder for them to keep their composure.

After people hear me share my story, they often ask "How can you tell such a moving story without breaking down yourself? It seems everyone was crying except you."

I have learned that as long as the audience sheds tears at least occasionally while listening to my story, I can get through it without crying. However, if I ever spoke about the deaths of my three sons and it did not move the audience to tears, I know I would fall apart. Their tears say, "We're with you. We hurt for you." Their tears give me strength.

Another stress area will be the holidays. Families may need to give themselves permission not to celebrate holidays in the same way they did before their loved one died. After the death of their eighteen-year-old daughter, one family I knew went on a picnic for Thanksgiving and took a trip over the Christmas holidays. It is important for the family to talk together and be allowed to express their feelings freely about upcoming seasonal holidays, birthdays, and anniversaries.

My mother died March 20, 1995. My parents' 59th wedding anniversary would have been October 18, 1995. As the day approached, my father said, "What should we do on the 18th?"

I asked what he wanted to do, and he said, "Well, you always took us out to dinner. I guess that's what I want to do."

I agreed we would take him out to dinner, but I suggested he meet me at Mom's grave first. My father came with a bouquet of flowers. I came with a bouquet of balloons. I explained that we were going to send the balloons off to heaven in memory of Mom. My father loved balloons, but he launched the first one rather hesitantly. "Look at her go," he commented as he sent the second one off into the heavens. As the third one drifted away, my dad waved and said, "Say hi to Bertie for me!"

As we went to dinner that evening, the waiter asked, "Are we celebrating a special event tonight?"

At first I said "no," but then I said, "Well, actually if my mother hadn't died last March, we would be celebrating my parents' 59th wedding anniversary. We aren't really celebrating, but we are *commemorating* a very special event in our lives." The waiter was very kind as he talked with my dad some about my mom. Then at the end of the meal, he brought a complimentary dessert with three spoons so that we could all enjoy it together.

On the first anniversary of my mom's death, my dad, my son, his wife, and their three children, and I all met at my mother's grave. I came with balloons for everyone. We built a beautiful memory that day, and we have wonderful pictures for the grandchildren's memory books of them and Great-grandpa Willett and their balloons.

As my father's health began to deteriorate, he started giving me instructions for his funeral which he referred to as "when I take off." He said, "When I take off, don't forget the balloons!"

At his memorial service in September of 1996, as each person left the sanctuary, they were given a helium-filled balloon. I sent mine up first and then 200 other balloons joined mine in a final "I love you!" to Mel Willett.

The next Father's Day our family gathered in my backyard to pay tribute to my grandchildren's two great-grandpas who died during that year. While we may not feel like celebrating, it is important that we commemorate important events and important people in our lives.

If you don't feel like celebrating Christmas or other holidays this year, don't be hard on yourselves. The world is not going to stop if you don't celebrate Christmas this year. Some of your extended family may feel frustrated, but try to explain as kindly and gently as you can that your heart is just not ready for big celebrations yet.

Our family traditionally celebrated Christmas on Christmas Eve, and because that was also Aunt Lucille's birthday, we always made it a double celebration. But after Aunt Lucille and Uncle Louie, my mom's sister and brother-in-law, died as a result of that explosion and flash fire, Mom wanted to cancel all of December. However, Christmas continued to come.

A friend of my mother's sent her a poem that expressed all our feelings. My mom put the poem in with a box of pictures and tucked it away. The December after Nate's death I was sorting through that box and found the poem. What timing!

Once again Christmas, a birthday, and the loss of a loved one were all mixed together. The poem was appropriate, even thirty-four years later, so I made copies of it and sent it to other bereaved friends.

"Merry" Christmas

I question if Christmas can ever be "merry,"
Except to the heart of an innocent child—
For when time has taught us the meaning of sorrow
And sobered the spirits that once were so wild,

When all the green graves that lie scattered behind us
Like milestones are marking the length of the way,
And echoes of voices that no more shall greet us
Have saddened the chimes of the bright Christmas Day—

We may not be merry, the long years forbid it,
The years that have brought us such manifold smarts,
But we may be happy, if only we carry
The Spirit of Christmas deep down in our hearts.

Hence I shall not wish you the old "Merry Christmas,"
Since that is of shadowless childhood a part,
But one that is holy and happy and peaceful,
The Spirit of Christmas deep down in your heart.

—Author Unknown

This can be a time to make some new memories and establish new traditions. It was four years after Nathan's death before I could do much Christmas decorating or have a real tree. That Christmas, Glen and I went out and cut down the biggest tree we could find. Since we had recently bought and refurbished a ninety-year-old Victorian house, I made many new decorations for our Christmas tree and did everything I could think of to use the Victorian theme all through the holidays.

To celebrate, Glen and I invited friends to go Christmas caroling with us. Several women friends joined me one afternoon for a Victorian tea and a brief piano and violin recital provided by one of my friends. These events took planning and effort on my part, and it wasn't always easy. Yet as we build new memories, we will become more confident that we can face the holidays and the future without our loved one.

Over the past few years I have collected rose motif Christmas ornaments for our tree. Each piece has a story; who gave it to me or where I purchased it. The rose theme gives me an opportunity to explain to my guests the significance of roses to me. I also had a florist design a Christmas centerpiece which includes three silk roses and three candles which we light for each special event during the Christmas season. We now also have a special candle to remember Grandma and Grandpa Willett.

Often after the death of a child or spouse, adults would be quite content to ignore the holidays, but they are forced to face traditional celebrations because of other children in the family. Friends can help in these situations by offering to take the children Christmas shopping, or to visit Santa Claus, or attend Christmas programs with them.

One family told me how they spent their first Christmas afternoon assembling a memory book of their deceased child. There were tears, of course, but they also spent a lot of time laughing as the pictures and notes brought back thoughts of the wonderful times they had had together. A family activity like this can help the children approach grieving in a healthy way.

It is important also for us to be sensitive when choosing Christmas cards for the recently bereaved. I was so relieved when I opened one envelope and read a card which said, "To Comfort You at Christmas." What a contrast to all of the jolly "Ho, Ho, Ho" cards that arrived in each day's mail. Writing a note to the bereaved family acknowledging that this holiday may be difficult and perhaps including a positive statement or story about the deceased will be appreciated.

My daughter and her husband did something very special to help us through our first Christmas after Nate died. Since Nate's birthday was Christmas Day, I was acutely apprehensive about it all. I invited many of our friends to spend the day with us, and I claimed the promise I had discovered many months before that God would give us "roses in December."

Christmas morning, my son-in-law, Mike, showed me a card he placed on the Christmas tree. It was addressed to Nate, but Mike handed it to me.

> Dear Family,
>
> Mellyn and I wanted to do something special this Christmas in thanksgiving to our Father for His incredible blessings upon us.
>
> It is our desire, if the Lord wills, to establish a tradition of Christmastime giving—a real sacrifice of ourselves for others, in memory of Nathan. Mike and Mellyn.

The first year they took a basket of food to a needy family and told the family they were doing this in memory of their brother, Nathan. The next year, they helped a Vietnamese family. A remembrance like that is a rose, a very special rose in December.

We adopted the same custom. For several years at Christmas we chose a boy to send to basketball camp in memory of Nate. I have also bought clothes for a child at the Children's Home Society and asked specifically that they be given to a teenage boy. One year, our friends Nancy and Peter sent a contribution to a Christian organization in Nate's name. We still do something special for someone each year in memory of our boys.

I am thankful for the friends who have stuck with us during these difficult years. Undoubtedly there were times when they were tired of hearing about Nate, the accident, the trial, the insurance, etc. They probably wondered if we would ever stop talking about our troubles, but they were patient and they let us talk. It was a very important part of our healing.

We don't talk about Nate constantly now. We are beginning to see him as "one of the children," not necessarily just as "Nathan who died." Our friends have learned to talk about him in a natural way, too. We can laugh about his funny and sometimes irritating habits, the times he did something wrong, his pet peeves, and all of the fun we had with him. He is beginning to take a normal spot in the history of the Heavilin family. Much of this normality has been regained because our friends have given us freedom to talk about him and work through our loss. They have also taken time to remember with us, for which we will be forever grateful.

If you have experienced a recent loss, let me encourage you to find friends with whom you can talk freely. Support groups can be helpful, also. Perhaps there is a group in your church which can meet your needs. If not, try to find a group such as The Compassionate Friends. Although they do not have a Christian emphasis, you will find people there who will understand your feelings and your frustrations.

If you have friends or coworkers with whom you feel strained because you can't share how you really feel, don't be too hard on them. If they are close friends, gently explain your needs. If they still don't respond, try to understand that their background and training may not free them to be as open as you would like them to be. Love them anyway, and let them learn from you. Perhaps they will observe enough that they will be able to pass your attitudes on to others even if they can't help you.

Thank God for all of the friends He gives you who do understand. They are beautiful, priceless roses.

The Rose of Friendship

A true friend is always loyal,
and a brother is born to
help in time of need.
PROVERBS 17:17, TLB

When I was a little girl, my father had hanging in his office a plaque which read, "He is rich who has two friends." After Nathan's death, God showed me that, regarding friends, I was a millionaire!

Most people going through a tragedy have more help than they need the first week or so. But soon the crowd thins out. The bereaved often ask, "Where are all those people who said they would help me?"

I was afraid that would happen in our case, but it didn't. Oh, of course, the crowd thinned out, but many people stuck with us.

When Nate died, my friend Donna Lynn was expecting her sixth child. She didn't have a lot of time to come to my house or take me to lunch, but her limited time didn't keep her from helping me. She helped by letting me help her.

She would call and say, "Marilyn, I need some typing done (or someone to watch the baby, or someone to be outside with her four-year-old). Will you come and help me?" After I helped her, we would have some time to talk. Donna Lynn accomplished two things with this approach. She helped me feel useful again and showed she cared by spending quality time with me. I'm glad she didn't let her busy schedule get in the way of helping a friend.

I didn't know Joan well before the accident, although her children were close friends of Nate's. That didn't stop her from coming to our house the very first morning and cooking breakfast for us. A few weeks later at church, Joan said, "Marilyn, I just want to tell you how much I appreciate it that you're letting the people in this church watch you grieve. You are open with how we can help you. You aren't trying to hide your feelings from us. We're a new church, and we need to learn how to work with people in crisis."

Then she went on to ask, "Would you be willing to meet me for lunch periodically so I can learn more from you?"

Her psychology was wonderful. She could have said, "Let me take you to lunch so that I can help you, honey." But she didn't. She put me in a position where I felt comfortable accepting her invitation. She didn't make me feel like a charity case.

When I accepted her offer, I had no idea of all we would be facing in the next few months. Many times I got so frustrated with the legal system, or the insurance situation, that I would think to myself, *If I can just hang on until Wednesday when I have lunch with Joan, I'll be OK.*

I knew I could be honest with Joan. I didn't have to be guarded about what I said. I could trust her with my deepest feelings. Through those very difficult months, Joan was my release valve. She helped me keep my sanity and a proper perspective on the situation.

During one of those lunches, Joan shared how Nate's death had affected her family. Her daughters Sue and Donna were so moved by his death that just going to the funeral, paying their respects, and helping us didn't seem like enough. As a family, they decided to do something which would involve them personally. For several weeks their family had a moratorium on television in memory of Nate. They felt if the whole country could do so in honor of a deceased president, the Morrill family could certainly curtail their television watching in honor of a friend.

Their act of sacrifice was very kind, but it meant even more because they shared it with us. The bereaved are encouraged when they know their loss is shared by others.

My friend Nancy was the first person we called after we heard about the accident. She came to the hospital immediately—a thermos of coffee in hand—and then came home with us and stayed until midnight Friday evening. Nancy and her husband Pete practically lived with us for the next two or three weeks.

Nancy made all of the phone calls we couldn't make; she helped arrange for food to be brought in; and she took care of our guests. Pete handled the logistics of such things as getting people from one place to another and bringing chairs from the church to our house after the funeral.

A few weeks later I discovered Nancy had done something even more special as she handed me a legal-sized note pad and a cassette tape. She said, "Here's the start of your book whenever you decide to write about this."

She went on to explain she had been taking notes for the past few weeks of everything that had been going on at our house: the people, the phone calls, the gifts, the cards, and our reactions. Then she had made a casssette tape of her personal feelings about Nate's death.

It was a long time before I could listen to the tape, and it was hard to imagine I would ever forget the details of those two weeks. But as I read the notes and listened to the tape about six months later, I discovered I had already forgotten much of what had happened. As time passes, I realize more and more how special Nancy's gift really was.

The best thing some of my friends did for me was just to let me cry. Sometimes, the minute I would hear a friend's voice, I would start to cry. My friends didn't condemn me; they simply let me cry.

My friend Diana is very sensitive to my needs, and she can tell when I am getting ready for a good cry. When I call and ask if she can meet me at my favorite restaurant for a piece of pie, she doesn't question me. She just says, "What time?" It is so comfortable to be with Diana because she freely admits she misses Nate, too. She doesn't just watch me cry; she cries with me. That's a true friend.

On the second anniversary of Nate's homegoing, my mother took flowers to the grave. She found a bouquet already there with a card which read, "Nate, we'll never forget you. See you later." It was from Diana and her family. Diana is a special bloom in our bouquet of December roses.

Friends can be sensitive to the needs of children in bereaved families by giving them extra attention, taking them places, or just listening to them. Frequently, the parents are so distraught themselves they are oblivious to the needs of the children.

Our son Matt had sat with his friend Roger the November before Nate's death when Roger's wife faced serious surgery. He carried food to Roger, ran errands for him, and was his sounding board. After Nate's crash, Roger was able to return the favor to Matt. He came to the hospital and then stuck with Matt during the remainder of the day.

In Matt's words, Nate had been his "social life" for several years. He had transported Nate and his friends to many high school events and even had driven them on the field trip to Los Angeles the day of the accident.

Roger recognized the empty space that Matt would need to fill and he helped by spending as much time with him as possible in the early weeks following the accident. Often bereaved brothers and sisters are forgotten, so we are grateful that Roger saw he could minister to Matt just by being there.

Our pastor was a special friend to us. Pastors often want to spend time with bereaved families, but their schedules won't allow for daily or weekly calls, and the families seem to get lost in the pool of good intentions. Our pastor found a way to keep in touch with us without spending a lot of time. The greatest thing he did was come as soon as we called. The week of the funeral he stopped by daily, but after that he called us each evening between 9 and 10. We both got on the phone for a three-way conversation with him which enabled us to hear each other's reaction to his questions.

He would ask, "How did it go today?" We would relate the happenings of the day.

"How do you feel about today's happenings?" Sometimes we felt good, and sometimes we didn't. Often we would shed a few tears with him.

"What's happening tomorrow?" We would relate our plans; perhaps we had a special meeting or a court date.

"Let's pray." We would join in conversational prayer, for the events of the next day.

"Now go to bed and get some rest." Often we went to bed simply because he suggested it. Sometimes we didn't seem able to make even those simple decisions for ourselves.

Those conversations usually took only five to ten minutes, but they met a vital need in our lives. The pastor communicated that he cared, and he also sensed if we had some special needs the church could meet.

In a large church, the pastor probably would not be able to make contact through a daily phone call, but he could assign an elder, deacon, deaconess, or another caring person to keep in touch with the family and serve as a link to himself and to the church.

A pastor's secretary could keep a card file, with notations such as: "Nate Heavilin died February 10, 1983; send Glen and Marilyn a card." This special touch would be greatly appreciated by the bereaved family.

Occasionally during the next few months a note would appear in our bulletin, "Remember to pray for the Heavilins as they continue to adjust to their recent loss." Our pastor was giving us time to grieve.

Later, recognizing the depth of understanding concern our pastor had seemed to feel, I began to suspect this was not common. I wondered if other grieving families were forced to deal with people who showed less care?

Feeling that I needed to know this, I sent a survey to about forty different families I had met over the past few years who had experienced the loss of a family member. I asked them to score their treatment by medical personnel, clergy, morticians, law enforcement agents, and lawyers. Along with medical personnel, the clergy got the lowest marks. Many of the families felt the clergy were unwilling to spend time with them and unable to answer their questions. Most commented that they seldom saw the clergy again after the funeral.

One friend related that about a month after his son's death, the pastor did call and ask, "How are you doing?"

Ben thought, *Finally someone is interested in us,* so he took the risk of answering honestly and said, "Well, pastor, we're really not doing very well. My wife and I are having trouble talking to each other, and I'm depressed most of the time."

There was silence. Finally Ben realized that the pastor couldn't handle his openness, so he pulled the mask of peace back over his heart and said, "Oh, really pastor, I'm just having a bad day. All in all, we're doing just fine."

The pastor muttered, "Well, I'm glad to hear that," and quickly ended the call.

Why would a pastor do that? First, because he has not been prepared to deal with the bereaved. Few seminaries deal with the subject of death except to teach future pastors how to conduct a funeral. Second, often when we are open with him and try to describe the hurt inside of us, he thinks we expect him to have a quick fix. Since he doesn't have a way to patch us up and take the pain away, he feels uncomfortable around us and finds it easier to stay away. When we say we're doing "just fine," he feels better and doesn't feel obligated to try to meet our needs.

Few of the bereaved are looking for a quick fix. It doesn't take us long to realize that our problem can't be taken care of quickly, and we don't really expect anyone to fix it. What we do need is knowledgeable people around us who will listen and at least discuss our questions with us.

One thing pastors can do is to be well versed on what their particular denomination teaches on the subjects of heaven, hell, and salvation. What is heaven like? Is my loved one there? What happens to babies when they die? If my loved one committed suicide or was involved in a terrible crime before he died, can he still go to heaven? Will we know each other in heaven? What part did God play in all of this?

Most bereaved people will appreciate a pastor who has thought through these issues, has come to some conclusions, and is willing to interact with his parishioners on these topics. Even a well thought out "I don't know" will be accepted if the family is certain the pastor cares.

I have spent a lot of time thinking about the sovereignty of God in the past few years. I have searched the Scriptures and formed what I hope are biblically-based opinions on that subject. However, when I have wanted to bounce my ideas off of someone else, I have had difficulty finding clergy who were willing to interact with me. I am very grateful to one pastor who shows real friendship and who has been willing to listen to me and read my writings to make sure I'm still on track. He hasn't judged me when my theories have seemed strange or out in left field; he has just patiently guided me toward what the Bible says.

When a loved one dies, even the unchurched and most non-religious people will start thinking about heaven and a life after death. It behooves pastors and churched people to be ready with some well-documented answers.

Although people want to help the bereaved, many times they simply don't know what to do. We had to be willing to make our needs known. Sometimes this was hard because we didn't want to admit we needed other people. But when we did, we found most people willing, and even anxious to help us.

There were days when the depression was so heavy I didn't have the strength to pick up the phone and call so someone could encourage me. On those days, I cried out to God and said, "God, I think I need help. If You agree with me, please have someone call me or contact me because I just don't have the strength to reach out to anyone today. If no one calls, then I'll know that You want me to work through this alone with You. I will trust You to meet my needs in the right way."

My prayer has always been answered, and I have received many calls from people stating, "I don't know why I'm calling, but God just keeps bringing you to my mind, so I had to call to see how you're doing." Other times I didn't receive any calls, but God would show me a Scripture, or lead me to a book, or give me a special thought that would lift my spirits and help me go on with life.

My friend Irene lives in Chicago, more than two thousand miles away, but she and I have become very sensitive to each other's needs. One day I felt a strong desire to call Irene. I tried several times, but no one was home. When I finally reached her late that evening, Irene heard my voice and burst into tears. She sobbed, "Oh Marilyn, Jonathan (her only child) is in the hospital and we don't know what's wrong with him."

After Irene shared more details with me, we were able to pray together and claim God's peace for Irene, Jonathan, and the rest of the family. Irene received comfort in the realization that if God cared enough about her to touch the heart of a friend thousands of miles away, then surely He was aware of Jonathan's needs and would care for him, too, which He did. A few days later, Irene took her little boy home.

When God puts someone on your mind, respond right away. God is most likely wanting to use you to respond to that person's immediate need. If you can't call or go to them, then at least take time to pray for them, asking God to meet their needs as He sees fit.

Recently I spoke at bereavement groups on two subsequent nights. Both groups presented me with beautiful bouquets of roses. I wanted to share my roses with someone who needed them, so I whispered a quick prayer, "Dear Lord, please bring someone to my mind who would really appreciate these roses today." The thought came immediately, *Take them to Nancy Hinkley.* Nancy is someone who was especially kind to my parents, so I liked the idea and thought, *Great! As soon as I finish at the beauty parlor, I'll come back home, get the roses, and take them to Nancy's office.* Then I went on with my day's schedule. As I finished at the beauty parlor, I looked up, and there was Nancy! I said, "I have a present for you." She smiled and said, "What a nice surprise! Are you giving me a gift because it's my birthday?" I had no idea it was Nancy's birthday, but God knew. He also knew she needed some roses in her life, and He used me to deliver them!

A friend will not force himself on those in need, but will be responsive to their needs. A faithful friend is a beautiful rose.

If you are the bereaved person, be willing to let your needs be known. When you're having a terrible day, don't be afraid to admit it. Call somebody and just say, "Help." If you are so discouraged you don't have the strength to ask for help from other people, remember God has promised He will always be with you.

"The Lord is nigh unto them that are of a broken heart; and saveth such as be of a contrite spirit" (Psalm 34:18).

Call on Him. He will hear, and He will answer. He wants to be your forever friend.

The Rose of Understanding

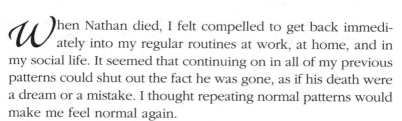

How much better is wisdom than gold,
and understanding than silver.
PROVERBS 16:16, TLB

*W*hen Nathan died, I felt compelled to get back immediately into my regular routines at work, at home, and in my social life. It seemed that continuing on in all of my previous patterns could shut out the fact he was gone, as if his death were a dream or a mistake. I thought repeating normal patterns would make me feel normal again.

So, less than two weeks after Nate died, I returned to my job at the high school where he had attended. The trip to school, Nate's and my private time together, had always been so much fun. Now, making the drive alone was horrible. I tried to listen to tapes, but I couldn't retain what I heard. The traffic made me nervous, and I felt nauseous as I drove past the wrecking lot where Nate's crushed car was stored.

Being at school seemed so strange: I had lost track of my purpose for being there. I walked into my office and all I could see was the chair where Nate had sat each morning. Since teachers had to arrive early, Nate usually studied in my office before school started. As I would look into my room from the doorway after the teachers' meeting, I could see this lanky boy, sprawled comfortably in a chair, his size-eleven feet propped on another chair. When I returned to work, that scene, still vivid in my mind, haunted me.

The first day back, I learned that two of my students had received highly coveted scholarships, the very ones I had worked on so enthusiastically the day of Nate's accident. Hearing they had won, I burst into uncontrollable sobbing. Two weeks earlier I would have been elated; of course, I was still happy for them, but my heart was breaking because as his counselor I would never get a chance to help my Nate win a scholarship. After two hours of trying to work, I went home.

Occasionally I tried to write my feelings:

> The fog still hasn't lifted. I move, I walk, I talk, but it is all automatic. There is little feeling. Sometimes the fog lifts and the feelings rush in. Then, all I can do is cry. It seems the only time I am real, reacting honestly, without guarding every word or look, I start to cry.
>
> When the fog lifts for a brief moment, it's as though someone just kicked me in the stomach. As I am reeling with the pain, my mind registers the one prevailing thought: Nathan is gone; NATHAN IS GONE. When I can't stand the pain anymore, my mind goes back into neutral, back into the fog.

Although I managed to continue working for the next two years, time didn't really improve the situation. Often I felt I was stumbling around in a dream; my mind wouldn't concentrate on any one thing for more than a few minutes. The extra-curricular activities—basketball, cross-country, ensemble—lost their meaning. There were constant reminders everywhere—scholarships, graduation, homecoming. Within a few weeks everyone else was back to normal, but Glen and I finally realized we had no normal to get back to. We had to learn a new normal, a normal without Nate.

Society needs to understand what trauma is and what it (especially an unexpected, traumatic loss) does to a person. We may look all right on the outside, but our minds do not function properly, and may not for months, or even years. I related to a young mother who had just lost a six-week-old child how sometimes I could not keep a thought in my head long enough to find a piece of paper and write it down. She exclaimed, "Oh thank goodness you have that problem, too. I thought I was losing my mind!"

Parents at The Compassionate Friends have shared that sometimes they are driving on the freeway and they can't remember where they're going. Others have called someone and when the person answers, they can't remember whom they were calling.

Many bereaved people change educational or vocational plans because they have lost the drive to go on in the same direction. These situations often don't improve in the first few months; it may be years before the person can remain constant in his lifestyle.

It helps if pastors, counselors, and friends understand that these reactions are normal. They can encourage the bereaved person not to give up but to try to discover if a temporary adjustment can be made. An extended leave of absence, a day off each week, or even a change to a part-time position may relieve the immediate pressure. Above all, they should help the bereaved person understand he should not feel guilty about being unable to function normally. The situation isn't normal after a death or other severe crisis, and it's OK to try to make things easier until life becomes more stable.

It was very difficult for me to continue in the teaching position I held at the school where Nathan had attended. People kept telling me it was important that I not quit, that I not *give up,* almost as though I would be letting everyone down if I changed jobs. I took every day of sick leave and vacation that I had available, and then I felt trapped. I felt I had no alternative but to trudge into work each day and *hang in there.* My mind would not help me come up with a solution to my problem. Then one of my friends said, "Well, just tell them to cut your pay, but you need more time off." What an insightful thought! Normally, I would have been able to figure that out for myself, but my mind had gone into neutral, and I felt completely out of control.

It's not unusual for people in crisis to feel they're in spiritual limbo. Even mature Christians may not have the mental strength to maintain normal Christian patterns.

When their only child, Robert, was killed in an automobile accident, Dick and Delores displayed amazing strength. The memorial service was honoring to the Lord and many lives were touched through it. But Delores recalls, "For three weeks after Robert's death I couldn't pray for myself but felt the power of others praying for me. After this period, I had a particularly bad day and was unable to cope. Then I realized that no one was praying, and God revealed to me that I now needed to express my own needs directly to Him."

The grief process takes a different path for each person, but it's important that he allow himself to grieve. No one who has lost a loved one is going to get a reward in heaven for trying to return to normality immediately as though the person never existed. Those who handle loss well are usually those who acknowledge their pain, admit to feelings of anger or bitterness, work through those feelings, and give themselves time to heal.

My friend Barbara discovered the importance of allowing herself to grieve through two loss experiences. She says,

> When our son was stillborn at full term, we were living in the country without a single house in sight. We were relatively new in the community and, though we were attending church occasionally, our roots were not deep. The church was without a pastor also. Our son was born in the same hospital and ward where I had been working as a nurse only weeks earlier so the nurses were my coworkers. A woman from our church also delivered the same day, and she and her healthy baby were across the

hall. None of our family lived close by. As I look back, I realize I was still playing the role of nurse—being concerned for everyone else's feelings and stuffing my own. I even helped the staff with their charting and so everyone felt I was doing "just great." No one visited us and my husband and the funeral director attended the baby's funeral all alone. My tears (and there were many) were saved for when the door was closed and it was safe—like at night when the staff was scarce and people thought I was sleeping.

Our families never discussed our loss. It was as though I had never even had a baby. My husband was extremely pleasant and kind but after a couple of weeks he, too, felt it was time to move on with life—and as a result those wounds never really healed.

It wasn't until twenty-three years later and the fire in which our house burned that I really understood the grieving process, and then quite by accident. We lost everything including our pet dog. Since the fire was considered a disaster and many of our friends also lost their homes or came close to losing them, people wanted to talk. We had calls from all over the United States, and many friends stopped by to visit and wanted to hear *everything*. At first I cried lots as they probed, but then it became easier and easier to handle and before long I realized that those wounds had healed well. It was OK to weep.

I also became aware of the reasons healing had not occurred those many years earlier. No one deliberately wanted to hurt us. It is just so difficult to probe and see someone struggle, and keep probing. However, it is essential if healing is to occur. Apparently people are more comfortable probing about things (such as fires) as opposed to the loss of a person, and I still struggle with that.

Another difficult step for some in the healing process is cleaning out the deceased person's room and distributing his possessions. There is no particular time after the death when it is best to do this, but I can tell you what was comfortable for me.

As I mentioned in the first chapter, when Jimmy died some well-meaning friends emptied our house of all reminders of Jimmy the very first day while I was out of the house, without my knowledge or consent. I came home to discover an empty bedroom, and I was enraged. I managed to conceal my feelings because I realized my friends had not intended to hurt me, but I felt they had trod on sacred ground. I needed to take care of Jimmy's things as a part of my grief work, and I needed to do it when it was comfortable for me.

When Nate died, the very next morning I knew that his new Nikes and his golf clubs should go to his brother-in-law, Mike. A stuffed musical dog from his childhood went to his girlfriend Sheila, and his gold monogram key ring went to Matt after we had it especially engraved on the back, "To a super brother."

A few weeks later I asked some of Nate's closest friends to come over and go through his closet and choose any clothing they would like. I gave some things to a cousin for her son and sent the remaining clothes to Goodwill. I saved Nate's sweat-suit, a football uniform we gave him when he was six, and a cowboy suit I had made for him when he was eight—they are for our grandchildren. When our grandson Nathan turned six, I presented him with the football uniform. He looked at it like he had discovered gold! I cried while I hugged him, but I'm so glad I saved it for him.

It was several months before I could go through Nate's drawers, desk, and notebooks. When the time came, I asked Mellyn to spend the day with me and help finish this heart-rending project. How or when you tackle those difficult assignments is up to you, but I would recommend you not try it alone. Find someone who shares your grief and can understand and share your memories and your tears.

As the friend of a grieving person, you may be able to identify stress points before he can. Let him know that it is all right to back away and say "I've had enough." That's not admitting defeat; it's using good sense. Often the grieving person cannot step outside of the situation enough to recognize when he's pushing himself too far.

My son, Matt, met a need in my life with a solution I didn't really appreciate at the time. He noticed I had difficulty with some of the phone calls I received, such as the lady who called to tell me what a nice man the drunk driver was and how much he liked children, or the agent from the loan company who called to make sure we were going to make the final payment on our mangled Toyota but never bothered to offer his condolences; so Matt bought me a telephone answering machine.

I had always hated those things—I found it irritating when I called someone only to have a little machine talk back to me. However, I knew Matt had done the right thing. Some days I wasn't up to talking to anyone, and I always seemed to have difficulty talking to the families of the other young people who had been in the accident or to anyone regarding the legal matters, so I decided to try the answering machine. Just knowing who was calling before I decided if I wanted to answer the phone was a great relief to me. Matt helped me in a situation where I seemed unable to help myself because I felt an obligation always to be available to others.

When you are hurting, it takes a lot of effort to try to help yourself, but the effort is worthwhile. Whether your new venture is traveling, joining a special interest group, or starting a project, although it won't take the hurt away, it will get you into the mainstream of life again, and slowly the hurt will become more bearable.

We need to understand that we may develop some idiosyncrasies we can't explain; they're just there. Several years after Nathan's death, Glen and I went to a baseball game with a group from our church. As we found our seats in Angel stadium, I exclaimed, "I can't sit in that seat. It's not on the aisle!" My pastor asked, "Why do you have to sit on the aisle?" I stumbled around for an answer and finally said, "I don't know. I just do." Later that evening I remembered why I always chose an aisle seat. The first Sunday I went back to church after Nathan died, I sat in the middle of a row in a very cramped auditorium. The congregation started to sing a chorus, and I realized the last time I sang that chorus, Nate was standing next to me. I began to sob and tried to bolt from the room. However, I had to stumble over about fifteen people to get to the aisle. That was the day I decided I would *always* sit on the aisle! I don't have to bolt very often anymore, but I still prefer an aisle seat.

It is important to understand that the bereaved may be in shock for a few days or a few months; they need to grieve; and they may have trouble in their jobs and in their family. The rose of understanding is one we all can acquire by being observant, listening to the bereaved, and responding to what we observe.

The interests or activities which help a bereaved person deal with his grief may seem strange to someone else; however, I believe bereaved people can do some rather unusual things and still be operating within the realm of normal. But I'm sure some of you are asking, "How can we tell if someone has moved outside the 'normal' limits?"

I am not a doctor or a psychologist, so I can only share with you the observations of a lay person who has experienced a great deal of grief and has talked with many people who are grieving. If a person refuses to acknowledge that someone is dead, keeps talking in the past, or continually seems to get the past and the present confused, I believe he needs professional help. If he becomes reclusive or deeply depressed, or if he openly talks of suicide, he should begin seeing a counselor.

I am reluctant to put time lines on grief because the healing process takes different lengths of time with each person, but you should be able to observe constant improvement. Even though improvement seems to come more slowly than you would like, if there is consistent progress, the person is probably doing all right. However, the healing might be accelerated if the person were to talk with a counselor or join a support group.

Christians often hesitate to seek professional help—they feel they shouldn't need it. But frequently that is exactly what they do need. It is important to get referrals and to choose a counselor carefully. If you are the grieving person, you should call the counseling center and inquire if they have counselors who deal specifically with grief therapy before you make an appointment.

The first hour I ever spent in a counselor's office occurred after my mother's death. I told the counselor, "I just need to have you check me out and see if you think I'm doing OK, because I'm not sure." I have only been back once since that time, but I do keep the counselor's number handy, just in case I need to give him a call.

I suggest that every bereaved family visit a therapist at least once. I think this would help each family member know that others in the family will be supportive if they decide to continue therapy.

Although Glen and I did not seek professional counseling, we did find great help through The Compassionate Friends. We found this group to be a safe place for us when we needed to feel safe.

This statement appeared in one of their recent newsletters;

> Our grief as parents of dead children is totally unique. Not even other bereaved parents can completely understand our grief. We are all individuals and we therefore grieve in our own very personal way. What we do have in common, though, is our loss. And that loss, no matter by what means, is very overwhelming. By our coming together we are able to share our pain and to come to the sad realization that we are not alone. At our meetings we discover other parents whose child died by similar circumstances. This will not erase our pain, but will help to support us.

In many areas there are support groups for people who have suffered specific types of losses, such people as widows, widowers, families of suicide victims, families of murder victims, and those whose children have died from Sudden Infant Death Syndrome. If you cannot find a group in your area, you may want to start one. Ask your pastor or the local funeral director for names of people who have had recent losses similar to yours. Call and invite them to have lunch with you or meet at your home for coffee. You very likely will find comfort in sharing your experiences and feelings with each other. You will be strengthened just by realizing you were able to help a fellow griever.

When you have experienced the death of someone close, or a divorce, or some other life-changing trauma, realize that your mind, body, and emotions have to adjust to this change. Read helpful books, tell others how you feel, make adjustments in your lifestyle to ease the stress, and ask God to help you learn valuable truths which you can share with others, so you, too, can be a beautiful rose of understanding to those around you.

The Rose of Innocence

But whoso shall offend one of these little
ones which believe in me, it were better
for him that a millstone were hanged
about his neck, and that he were
drowned in the depth of the sea.

MATTHEW 18:6

*W*hen a crisis comes, as adults we tend to get involved in dealing with our own grief, and many times the children in the family are put in the care of a close friend or relative until "things have returned to normal." Whether children attend the funeral or not, it is important for someone to be available to answer their questions and meet their needs.

When our Jimmy died of crib death in 1964, our daughter Mellyn was almost three years old. Jimmy's crib was in Mellyn's room. Glen went in to check on the children and discovered the baby was dead. For the next few minutes our attention was focused on Jimmy. Finally, I realized that Mellyn was still in the room, and she was huddled against the wall on her bed. Her first words were, "I didn't hurt Jimmy."

I assured her I knew she had done nothing wrong and told her an angel had taken Jimmy to heaven to be with Jesus. Months later I awoke in the night aware of a little hand moving across my face. Mellyn looked so relieved when she saw me move, and she said, "I just wanted to see if God took you, too." Words that had been comforting to me had been discomforting to a three-year-old.

After Jimmy's death, Mellyn reverted to baby talk and many babyish mannerisms. She often climbed up on my lap and said, "I'll be your baby now." It was two or three years before we felt Mellyn was a relaxed, carefree little girl again.

My brother was only two when his parents died and my parents adopted him. He can't really remember his birth parents nor the events surrounding the tragedy, but for many months afterward he would scream with fear when my mother left him with anyone else. He may not have been able to remember what had happened, but he definitely remembered the feelings of fear when his mommy and daddy left and never came back.

A pamphlet distributed by MADD (Mothers Against Drunk Driving) states:

> A child of two can sense loss and suffer the feelings that go with loss, but he cannot understand what death is. The child will pick up on the grief and anxiety in his surroundings and will need touching or holding. Explanations, however, will not be understood. The child this young can only understand that someone is present or not present.
>
> What one does is far more important to the child this young than what one says. Generally, it is best done with large doses of tender loving care—holding, cuddling, and stroking.
>
> A child between the ages of four to six may talk of the death of the person in the same detached way that he may talk of the death of a pet. This may be disturbing to the adults around him and their reaction may be confusing. Crying may be more out of confusion about what others are experiencing rather than the death itself.
>
> Most commonly, seven- or eight-year-olds become fearful of death because they realize for the first time that it is real....Some of their questions may indicate fears of their own death. Death can now be seen as an attacker who takes life. Although able to accept the finality of death,

many of the factors of early childhood still apply. It is important for children of this age to express their sadness, anger, fear, and guilt.[1]

Mellyn was four and a half when Ethan died, and I was very concerned about how she would react since Jimmy's death had been so difficult for her. However, she surprised us all. When she was told of Ethan's death, she commented, "That's OK, I've still got Nathan!"

When my grandmother died just two months later, Mellyn heard me say how bad I felt because Grandma never got to see Nathan.

She asked, "Is Grandma in heaven?"

When I said yes, she concluded, "Well, Ethan was Nate's identical twin, so he looks just like Nate. If Grandma's in heaven, she has seen Ethan, so she knows what Nate looks like."

She played with her toys a few minutes and then asked, "Do you have another grandma in heaven?"

I said, "Yes, my Grandma Empey."

With the beautifully innocent faith of a little child, Mellyn said, "Then she can have Jimmy."

Through Mellyn's faith she allowed me to see a picture of two grandmas rocking their great-grandchildren in heaven.

I personally feel it is good for children to be involved with as much of the grief experience as they are comfortable with, but it should not be forced. One family I know has experienced the deaths of three immediate family members in the past year. After the third death, the ten-year-old child said, "I can't go to another funeral," and the parents made the wise decision to let her stay home.

When a child dies, the siblings may feel guilty because God didn't take them instead of their brother or sister since, from their point of view, the one who died was the smart one, or the cute one, or Mom or Dad liked him or her better. A younger child may try to take the place of an older child by assuming his responsibilities, moving into his room, or wearing his clothes. Parents need to assure this child that they like him just as he is and they don't want him to be an imitation of someone else.

Young people also may take undeserved responsibility for the death. I met a young boy whose sister died by suicide. When the sister had attempted suicide previously, the brother had determined he was going to stay with her and watch her so that she could never try suicide again. However, one day when the boy had to leave the house for a legitimate reason, the sister took the opportunity to kill herself. My young friend was filled with self-imposed guilt: "If I had just made her go with me, this would not have happened." The parents' reassurance was not enough in this case. The boy needed an outsider's perspective to help him work through his grief and realize his sister's death was not his fault before he could forgive himself.

Sometimes the remaining child will display anger because his life has been disrupted or because all of the attention seems to be focused on the dead instead of the living. He may need help in getting the right assessment of his own importance. We also need to be careful how we talk about the deceased child. We may tend to talk only about his good qualities and not acknowledge his faults to the point that the remaining children begin to feel inferior and less important than the absent child. Being aware of this potential problem can help us avoid it.

When my aunt and uncle were fatally injured in the gas stove explosion, I was twelve. My parents considered leaving me with a babysitter while they drove to the hospital in Northern Michigan, but I begged them to take me along. I did not want to be separated from my family. If we were facing trouble, I wanted us to face it together.

We arrived at the motel late in the evening and my grandparents filled us in on the details of the accident. Grandpa took my parents to the hospital and I crawled into bed with Grandma. It was the middle of the night when Grandpa walked in and said, "Louie's dead!" I can still feel my Grandma's tears falling on me as we sat on the edge of the bed and she held me so tightly.

Early the next morning we all went to the hospital to sit with my Aunt Lucille. Everyone was allowed to go into her room except me because I was not old enough, so I sat in the waiting room alone most of the day. Frequently my father came out to give me a report. One report was: "Lucille is now unconscious; we don't think she'll live much longer." Later that afternoon, Lucille died.

When the family went to see Lucille's children in the burn ward, the doctor said I could not go. I started to cry and said, "Are they dying, too?" My mother finally convinced the doctor I needed to see the children and know they were all right. My fears were relieved when I was able to talk with the children. I am thankful my parents were honest with me, and I am so very glad they sensed my emotional need to see the children.

During the week of the funeral, people came to the house to talk with my mom and dad and my grandparents, but I don't remember anyone talking specifically with me. When I returned to school, my teacher came up to me, put her arms around me, and asked me how I was doing. The tears flooded my eyes, and she held me while I sobbed. I finally felt free to express my grief.

A bereaved sibling who attended The Compassionate Friends stated, "This is the first time anyone has asked, 'What happened to you?' Finally, someone has acknowledged that my brother's death didn't just happen to my parents; it happened to me, too."

Take time to seek out the children in a bereaved family. If they don't want to talk, then just play a game, read a book, or watch a favorite TV program with them. Children often feel that if bad things happen to them it must mean they are bad. As a friend or family member, you can help preserve their feelings of self-worth by spending time with them, hugging them, and praising them for their accomplishments.

Continuing normal patterns as much as possible will help give a child a feeling of security. One friend whose father was killed on the mission field when she was seven remembers the birthday party her mother prepared for her just two days after her father's death as one of the nicest parties she ever had. I'm sure that party was difficult for her mother, but it helped the little girl feel there were still some traditions and some people she could depend on. As a teenager, she also remembers feeling sad as she watched other girls being kissed by their dads, but she is grateful for her two brothers who gave her lots of special attention and many hugs.

A boy whose father has died needs the attention of a man, someone who will take him to a ball game or sit in the stands and cheer for him while he plays on the school team, confirming that he is a person of value.

The program at a recent The Compassionate Friends convention included a special panel for bereaved siblings. The most common complaint from the young people was how fearful and over-protective their parents had become since their brother or sister's death. The parents' fear is understandable, but it is important to give the remaining children freedom to live normal lives. At least be open with them. "Since your brother died in a car accident, I'm nervous about letting you take the car. I'll do a lot better if you make every effort to be home on time and always call if you are delayed."

Several summers after Nate's accident, a ten-year-old girl stayed with us for two weeks. One evening she went bike riding with some friends. While they were gone, we heard several sirens in our area. I got so nervous, I was almost in tears by the time the girls returned. I told her that those sirens reminded me of the sirens I heard the night Nate died, and silly as my reaction may seem, I would really feel better if she only went riding when Glen or I could go with her. Once she understood my feelings, she accepted my request quite willingly.

Getting over your fears and giving children room to enjoy life will take a while, but if you're honest with them, they will be more likely to cooperate with you.

Teenagers may have a particularly difficult time dealing with the death of someone close. Because of their youth, their grief is often minimized by adults, yet teenagers are old enough to feel the pain very deeply and also to feel the pain of others. While grieving for Nathan, I discovered that when I shared my feelings with some of his teenage friends, they were able to empathize with me better than many adults. The young people at Nate's school weren't afraid to acknowledge their grief. They were the ones who thought of giving me the roses at graduation and presenting the slide show at baccalaureate. They dared to speak openly about their love for Nathan and how much they missed him. I often received notes like these:

> I just wanted to take this time to tell you that I'm still thinking of you and praying for you. I hope my smile and questions of how you're doing make your days easier. Let me know if you need someone to talk to or to do something for you. Mickey

> When I see you in the halls, I can see that you are having a very hard time. I want you to know that if there was anything in the whole world that I could do that would lessen your hurt, I would gladly do it. When I see you hurt, it just hurts me so much inside I can hardly stand it. I can now truly understand 1 Corinthians 12:26 [NIV] that talks about the body of Christ: "If one part suffers, every part suffers with it; if one part is honored, every part rejoices with it." We all hurt with you, Mrs. Heavilin! Natalie

On the first anniversary of Nate's death, I received this note from one of my former students.

I just wanted you to know that I was thinking about you today. I know this must be a difficult time for you. Nathan was very special to all of us, and even though I miss him greatly, I'm sure I can't begin to understand the depths of your love for him and the mixed emotions you must have at this time. I only pray that God will continue to comfort you with the awesome fact that Nathan beat the rest of us home!
Andy

We need to be careful not to rebuff young people's attempts to express their sorrow. Sometimes we can help them by verbalizing feelings they might be having. "When an older brother dies, sometimes a younger brother can feel very lonely. He might even be mad at his brother because he left so suddenly. Do you ever feel like that?"

If our children don't seem comfortable sharing their feelings with us, we need to help them find someone they can talk to—school counselor, teacher, pastor, youth worker, grief counselor, or peer.

Reach out to bereaved children: Spend time with them and find out how they're feeling. They are innocent, fragile rosebuds who need gentle, loving care. Be a rose and help them through this difficult, confusing time.

The Rose of Hope

Now faith is the substance of
things hoped for, the evidence
of things not seen.
HEBREWS 11:1

*I*n the past few years, our son, Matthew, sometimes has joined Glen and me as we speak to bereaved families. Matt's perspective as a bereaved sibling has always been well received. Someday it is my hope that Matt and I will be able to write a book together on family grief. But for this time, I just asked for a chapter. Matt has a unique perspective in that he became a bereaved sibling at the ages of four, six, and nearly twenty-four, and is now the father of three, two of whom nearly died at birth. So it is with great pride that I present my son, Matthew Warren Heavilin.

While many bereaved parents feel, perhaps justifiably, the frustration of being only a spectator in the services for their son or daughter at the time of death, these parents may not be fully aware of the extra row of spectator seats, set just behind their own. This is where the siblings are ushered in to sit, too far back to reach out and touch, and left with only whatever view they can manage over their parents' shoulders.

The vast majority of siblings in that second or third row of onlookers are waiting for an invitation to step forward and participate as a younger member of the grieving family. Too many times, that invitation is never extended—the surviving children are overlooked in the overwhelming chaos. I personally believe that the vast majority of grieving parents and adult family members deliberately try to shield these little ones whom they love and cherish from the pain of the family tragedy.

However, a loss within the family forces us all, including children and young adults, to make adjustments, perhaps drastic revisions to the expectations, hopes, and dreams we have held in our hearts. No young person can endure such an experience without some basic loss of innocence; there is an intrinsic sobering effect. Even the youngest will absorb some of the confusion and frustration surrounding them, a confusion that responds poorly to lengthy explanations, but is calmed by an affectionate cuddle or a gentle hand.

Young adults can be caught in a conflict between their desire to stay involved and their desire to maintain their independence. And siblings of all ages feel an increased burden of personal responsibility to care for and protect their family, especially their parents, as they strive to find stability in their home.

When a parent loses a child, it is critical to remember that the entire *family* has suffered this loss.

I must admit that the family funerals (plural) of my early childhood are somewhat jumbled in my memories. It is difficult for me to place the details in proper sequence, even to this day. Silver and black limousines, or they may have been gold. Lacy white caskets that were smaller than me. Dressing in our best clothes when I knew it was not Sunday. My family sitting together, in a separate room, off to the side, hidden behind a pale curtain. Heart-shaped grave markers, flat and metallic. A set of knitted booties, bronzed and made into bookends. But all the vague images recalled more than forty years later still crystallize into one very clear thought, evident even then to a five-year-old child: *This is an important event, but it is not about me, and no one here has told me where I fit in.*

Even at that age I was looking for solid direction, and as the firstborn, I could sense that my line of command had taken a direct hit. In my innocence, I questioned the adults around me, "What are we supposed to do now?" It had not yet occurred to me that they were probably asking themselves the very same thing. But I persisted in my questions, and someone at last offered an answer, one that I got repeatedly with great conviction and compassion from at least three different adults (not my parents) in at least as many different scenes, "Don't worry. We'll get you ice cream."

Almost two decades later I again found myself dressed in coat and tie, wearing my Sunday best as it were, sitting in the hallway of a mortuary. I was now twenty-three and the last of my brothers, Nathan, lay in state just a few yards away. Through the years I had gained intellect, perception, and observation skills, but I had lost innocence, blind trust, and a willingness to accept people and events at face value. The typical maturity and understanding I had accumulated had made me better equipped to share in my parents' frustration, confusion, and feelings of helplessness. Growth had granted me the tools necessary to identify with my bereaved parents' grief, but Nature itself had robbed me of the congenital defense mechanisms that had served their purposes when I was only five.

In regard to the loss of my brother Nathan, I could see my own parents making a deliberate effort to keep me involved. We were very close to wrapping up the services when my father spoke to me directly, "Your mother and I have got to get out of here. I need you to stay behind and see to it that everything is taken care of." My orders had finally arrived, and I was determined to see them through.

However, as I reviewed the scene before me, for all my effort, I couldn't find a single task that had been left unattended. In every case, a courteous professional was doing his job. I eventually rounded up my brother's classmates, piled them into several cars, and we all ended up at Baskin-Robbins. It was smack dab in the middle of February, but I seemed to recall someone mentioning once upon a time that ice cream was therapeutic in these situations.

Just ten years ago, on a mid-winter Monday morning, a telephone operator cut in on an important business call I had made. It was Grandpa. He said only, "Grandma is gone." For one brief moment I felt a debilitating fear. I had been here before, and I just didn't know if I could do it again. I held my breath for an instant, not knowing what to expect, and then made myself one simple promise: *I will remember that this death is a part of my family's life.*

The viewing was held in the large chapel at the local mortuary. Amid the old friends and family paying their respects and sharing old stories, were my children, all three of them. Along with their cousins, they were playing tag, playing hide-and-seek, playing house, playing whatever games came to mind, because playing is simply their prime directive. Someone teaches children this somewhere: *Lacking any other direct orders from HQ, always resort to playing.*

Before long one of them discovered that secret room, just off to the side, behind the thin white curtain, all quiet and dark. At first the kids were not certain if this area might be off limits. I walked over and sat down behind the curtain.

Kids: "What is this room for?"
Matt: "Well, it's for us."
Kids: "Why?"
Matt: "So we can be alone."
Kids: "Why should we be alone?"
Matt: "So we can cry."
Kids: "Do we have to stay in here to cry?"
Matt: "I guess not."
Kids: "Can we cry out there?"
Matt: "I don't see why not."
Kids: "If we're in here, do we have to cry?"
Matt: "I don't think so."

Kids: "Can we open the curtains and stay here and still cry?"
Matt: "Yes, I guess so."
Kids: "Can we close the curtains again?"
Matt: "Sure."
Kids: "Can we crawl underneath these benches?"
Matt: "I'm sure *you* can."
Kids: "OK, so what do we do next?"
Matt: "Well, what do we always do next whenever we see Grandma?"
Kids: "We eat!"
Matt: "Of course we do. Let's go eat."

Questions left unanswered remain as questions to be raised again. The youngest of children can detect a dodge offered in place of an explanation. Offer your children the truth as you know it, in terms they can comprehend. Participation promotes a healthy grieving process. And in this regard, it may be the thought that counts most. Parents should watch for age-appropriate opportunities for their grieving children to participate. Your child may not yet possess maturity sufficient to address the full impact of the tragedy in your home. But the Creator has gifted the young with the emotional strength necessary to carry that burden to a later date when the more complex issues of life and death may be considered.

Life experience is an excellent teacher, but raw information, the memory of an event, or the recollection of an historical fact must be absorbed and applied to our personal lives to be of use. The problem here is timing, a factor beyond our control. This process of understanding and application will proceed at various rates for various family members. In order for a marriage to survive such a tragic loss, a husband and wife may be forced to reconcile, and to a certain degree, appreciate the differences in their personal grieving. But sometimes they fail to recognize similar differences in their surviving children.

My eldest son, Nathanael, is roughly the same age today that I was when I experienceed bereavement. These days he is very concerned about his several great-grandparents who have gone on to heaven, as well as his elders who remain here with us. Some nights I find him crying in his bed when he should be sound asleep. So I sit there in the dark with him and we talk and we share our thoughts and our hopes and our fears and our dreams. We talk about recognition because Nathan wants Grandma to be remembered. We talk about rituals and traditions because Nathan wants to know why we do what we do. We talk about reality because Nathan wants to know the truth. We talk about responsibility because, almost more than anything else, Nathan wants to know what is expected of him. And I tell Nathan every last thing that I know because I promised my grandmother I would not neglect The Blessing of the Generations. But when the questions just get too tough, or the nights just get too long, or the answers just don't seem to come easily, I promise him with great conviction, "Don't worry, son. We'll get you ice cream." He seems to understand.

Never risk giving your child an answer you do not personally believe. Be prepared to admit it when you don't have the answer to a small child's questions. You will maintain your personal integrity with maturing children when you acknowledge your own doubts.

At the most fundamental level, the best thing a bereaved parent can do for a surviving child is to tend to his or her own personal healing process. The objective here is for the child to see his parents happy again.

In the days immediately following the loss of a sibling, the surviving child observes his parents in mourning. As days pass, and barring outside interference, the child will invariably return to what appears to be "normal" much more easily and much more rapidly than the parents. Over time, though, siblings of almost any age may conclude that their dead brother or sister was the secret ingredient to their parents' happiness. In other words, *My parents cannot be happy without my brother, and now that he's gone, my parents will never be happy with me.*

Whether by rational reasoning or simple parental instinct, my own folks had a strong inner sense that led them to repeatedly remind their remaining children, "Regardless of what we may have lost, we are so thankful that you are still here with us." Simple words, but they helped us tremendously. These words, shared easily in ordinary times, may be muffled and obscured in the commotion following the loss of a child, so it is critical also that at least some portion of your actions attest to your words. This will give your remaining child a concrete basis for hope for the future.

A surviving sibling will likely take active steps to protect and care for his parents during their bereavement. In my own case I quickly reasoned, *If Mom always cries when she gets calls from the attorneys, buy her an answering machine. Those college application forms that keep arriving in the mail are certain to upset the folks, so let's get to the mail first and be sure to toss them out. Since there's no one at the house now to take out the trash, I'd better pick that up too. Mom and Dad need to get away, but the family car is at the wrecking yard. Better rent them one for the week.*

This self-appointed assignment is not so much duty as it is self-preservation. The surviving sibling still needs a family to be a part of. But the family he desires is broken, and to some it may appear irreparable. Still, the average child will rediscover hope much sooner than his parents. To a certain degree he has no choice. Although to hope again is to risk again, and that may be difficult, to continue without hope is not a viable option for a young adult.

In the fall of 1987, Debbie, my bride of three years, and I were anticipating our first child. Expectations ran high. We had every reason to be hopeful, and we were. We would have our first baby home before Christmas!

While Debbie's labor began normally enough at home, the doctors and nurses recognized that something was wrong the moment my wife entered the maternity ward. Just minutes after the nurse activated a bedside cardiac fetal monitor, that single, jagged black line went flat and the numeric display dropped to zero. Nine months worth of a healthy pregnancy, and just at this moment the baby's heart had suddenly stopped. Without looking back, the medical team wheeled the entire bed out the door and into an empty delivery room. As I dutifully trailed along behind, someone yelled, "Keep him out of here!" and I was left standing in the hall.

The doorway remained open, but I was left at the threshold, an odd spot for the father-to-be. Two nurses held a bluish-green drape across Deb's chest. Our young doctor, consistently enthusiastic in every previous meeting, seemed uncharacteristically subdued. The nurses simply looked frightened. It hadn't occurred to me that the anesthesiologist had not yet arrived. Fortunately, it had not occurred to Debbie either. A single direct shot of Novocain, a quick move of the knife, and the surgery had begun. Someone helped me to a chair.

I was confused, but I did recognize the nurse's voice; it literally pounded in my ears. "Respiratory Therapist to Maternity, STAT!" It seemed I was the only person in the ward not moving or not yelling. Well, there was me, and there was the baby, both quite still, both quite silent. I remember thinking to myself, *I wish someone would shut off the annoying PA system, "Respiratory Therapist, STAT!"*

He came flying past me. We'd never met, but I saw something there in that brief instant that was frighteningly familiar. No single part of his clothing fit him the way it had been intended. He wanted to be there already, but he was moving too quickly for a slippery waxed floor, and as he slid past the doorway, he briefly lost his balance and momentarily caught my eye. In that one glance an instant recognition triggered ancient memories buried deep in my mind. A little voice echoed back to me, "It's too late."

I was not yet five years old, and it was springtime in Indiana where my family lived. Dr. Walker sat in our living room checking out my weeks-old new baby brother, Jimmy. I knew

Dr. Walker because he gave me shots at his office, and because I saw him every Sunday at church, and because he lived just around the corner from our big new house, and because I played in the backyard and in the big cornfields with his two youngest boys. Mom thought maybe Jimmy was beginning to get sick. But that was no big deal because Dr. Walker lived right in our neighborhood, and Dr. Walker could stop by on his way home from work, and Dr. Walker was a real Doctor. I knew everything was fine. No reason to be worried. We all slept very well.

It was early morning, but it was light, when my dad put my little sister into my bed and told us both to stay still and stay quiet. But the house was alive, and we seemed to be the only things not moving and not yelling. And then Dr. Walker came flying past me. No single part of his clothing was on him the way it had been intended. He wanted to be there already, but he was moving too quickly for a slippery waxed floor, and as he slid past the doorway, he briefly lost his balance and momentarily caught my eye. In that one glance there was an instant recognition: It's too late. I was not yet in kindergarten, but already I knew that grown-ups were never supposed to look that scared, especially grown-ups who were doctors. It seemed a desperately long time, but I'm sure it had been really just a few minutes when my very weary-looking father came in and tried to explain to his two remaining preschoolers that God had unexpectedly taken little baby Jimmy to heaven during the night. At just four years of age, I couldn't grasp all the theological implications, but one lesson was perfectly clear and never ever forgotten: Doctors cannot always fix people's bodies when they break, and that includes even little babies.

So, twenty-five years later, I sat alone in the hallway, my lifeless child just a few feet away, and I wondered to myself, *Am I today following in my own father's footsteps? I am old enough now that I shouldn't be playing childish games. Life has taught me what these ER scenes are all about in the real world. It is simply too late.*

But a childhood is not composed of just one single lesson, or one single event. In the back of my mind I could hear my own five-year-old voice reciting a little snippet from a common Sunday school curriculum, "And now abide these three, faith, hope, and love."

Well, I have always had a studious predisposition, and I have no trouble reconciling children's lessons with my personal experience as an adult, so long as we keep the theories couched comfortably in an academic setting. By the time I had turned twenty-four, I had buried all three of my younger brothers. Jimmy had merely been the first to fall. But the experience of loss had only accentuated the sincere feelings of love, no part of which was ever diminished by a brother's departure. As the doctors labored, and I contemplated this innocent child's fate, I had no lack of love for my own offspring. I could say with sincerity, I am constrained by love for this unnamed child, and I am convinced of my faith in this unseen God. But on that particular day, October 24, 1987, just about 10:00 AM on a Saturday morning, sitting very alone on a folding chair in the hallway of this hospital, I experienced a life-and-death struggle with the concept of hope.

What I wanted was to have been at the hospital a day earlier. What I wanted was a fully staffed medical team ready and waiting to perform emergency procedures the moment we had arrived. What I wanted was for all these medical professionals to stop screaming at each other. What I wanted more than anything else in the whole world was to hear my own baby cry. But I was not certain if all the losses I had suffered in years past and all the lessons I had learned standing over caskets that were much too small could now justify my standing up one more time and facing this tragedy-in-the-making with a heartfelt hope.

And I wondered to myself, *Is hope doomed to be only a feeling, or is it possible that hope could be a choice?*

If hope had to be a feeling, then I was clearly coming up short. I did not feel hopeful. It was not natural for me. But, if hope could be a choice, then I at least had a chance. I decided that for me, for my family, on this day, hope would be a choice.

Eventually, a weary-looking doctor came out and tried to explain. He said, "Mr. Heavilin, I don't know you and I don't know how you feel about these sorts of situations. As doctors, we do everything we can, but beyond a certain point, it is simply up to God. Your little girl was clearly beyond that point." No pulse, no muscle tone, no brain activity. An Apgar score of zero for fifteen minutes. Beyond a humble doctor's reach, perhaps, but never beyond the reach of my God, and always within the realm of hope.

I didn't get to hear my baby's cry that morning; because it was days before they could remove the ventilator tubes, and even at that point it was really only a faint squeak, not truly a baby's cry. But with a little faith, and a willingness to hope, it became a sound of great promise.

I visit my brothers' gravesides, and I am struck with a love that longs to see their faces again. I contemplate my brothers' fate and I study and evaluate my personal faith. But my little girl, Katherine Nate, is in college now, and I cannot look at her face or hear the sound of her voice and not thank God for the gift of eternal hope.

The rose of hope is a rose we all need. Hope that we'll live through this awful nightmare; hope that God won't give up on us; hope that somehow our family will remain intact no matter how devastating our loss has been. Ask God to fill you with His hope.

The Rose of Uniqueness

I will praise thee; for I am fearfully and
wonderfully made: marvellous are thy works;
and that my soul knoweth right well.

PSALM 139:14

*W*hen I first met Glen Heavilin, I knew I had met my perfect match. He was quiet, steady, and dependable. He
thought through everything he did, and he didn't speak until he
had something important to say. He was all the things I wasn't!

He listened quietly while I talked on and on, and he was
content to let me get involved in lots of committees and social
groups while he stayed home and studied or watched the children. His mood was predictable—peaceful and happy—while
mine constantly changed. He provided me with dependability
and I provided him with variety.

It really has been a good match. We've had very few major
arguments. I have disagreed with him often, but I soon discovered it was no fun to argue with someone who wouldn't argue
back. So we began to do it Glen's way—we reasoned with each
other and settled things peacefully. His way worked just fine
until Nathan's death.

We were grieving differently, and our marriage was severely
tested. It hadn't been that way with the deaths of Jimmy and
Ethan, and we knew we now had to find out what the problems
were. Before, our strength had been in our love, our concern,

and our admiration for each other. After Nate's death those things didn't seem to be enough. We disagreed on everything and we couldn't understand why.

With the other boys' deaths, there was no one to blame, there were no legal hassles. With Nate's death, waiting for all the legal and insurance matters to be settled was like waiting for the benediction at the funeral, and it slowed down the healing process. Going to court again and again, only to find the trial date has been postponed can be like a hammer blow driving you lower and lower into the depths of despair.

Our case was postponed eleven times and then actually was settled on the one day we didn't go to court because the district attorney felt the trial would just be postponed again. We felt cheated. We did not have a chance to hear the man declared guilty; nor did we have a chance to speak regarding his sentencing—one more frustration in the long line of bewildering legal proceedings.

An organization such as MADD, Mothers Against Drunk Driving, could have given us professional help, but there was no chapter in our area, and we were too tired and confused to try to get help anywhere else. I wish a counselor or a friend had been able to do that for us.

Having to deal with the manslaughter case was very discouraging because we felt uninformed and excluded. I have since begun to understand that in a criminal court, the victim and the victim's family have no actual representation. The district attorney represents the state, but not the victim. The defendant can hire as much representation as he can afford, or the state will provide a public defender to represent him. However, we, as Nathan's family, had no one to represent us in the criminal case. No one volunteered any information; we had to dig to find out what was going on. No one in the DA's office really cared to know much about Nathan. When the case was finally resolved, the drunk driver was sentenced to three years probation and not a day in jail. Agreeing to the terms of the plea bargain was the DA's decision, not ours.

If you are a pastor, or counselor, or friend of the bereaved person, please understand that that person needs to express his feelings in whatever way is comfortable for him without fear of condemnation. I was angry at a justice system that in my opinion didn't hand out a punishment equal to the crime, and I became quite cynical. Some of my feelings were quite negative, yet I still needed to express them. But when people responded with, "You're a Christian; you shouldn't feel like that," I was devastated.

I thought, *It's true that I'm a Christian, but I'm still having these feelings. Is there something wrong with me?* It was much more helpful when someone let me say how I felt and then worked with me to resolve those feelings without condemning me.

Just recently a family called me to ask if I thought it was all right for them, as Christians, to attend the trial of the person who killed their child. They thought it might appear vengeful because they wanted the killer to pay for his crime. That isn't vengeance. Vengeance would be if the victim's family harrassed the defendant or defied the decisions of the court. However, we live in a land where it is unlawful to kill someone, and our courts declare there is a consequence to breaking the laws. What better place for those Christian parents to be than right there in court every day to represent their deceased child and also to be a physical reminder that they uphold the laws of the land. At the same time, that means if the court finds the defendant not guilty or gives him a lighter sentence than seems fair, they honor the court in that decision, too.

In regard to the insurance, we felt vulnerable because we had so little control. Our objective was to get the insurance settled as soon as possible. The amount of the settlement concerned us to a point—we felt it had to be adequate because to us it represented Nate's "worth," and we could not accept the possibility we might receive less because he was "not an only child" or because he was "only seventeen." On the other hand, it didn't have to be exorbitant; we had few bills to pay, and we were not dependent on Nate for financial support.

The other families felt they needed plenty of time to make sure the doctors had discovered all of the injuries their children had incurred—the larger the settlement, the more they would have available to "protect their child's future." This was hard for us since Glen and I had discovered years ago that only God can protect our children's future.

We realized their goals were different from ours, but Glen's reaction to that was opposite to mine. He felt we had no choice but to wait since our insurance company did not want to settle with us until they could settle with everyone. He even suggested we should wait patiently!

Well, I waited because I had no choice, but I certainly didn't wait patiently. I fussed and fumed. I wanted Glen to call the other families and demand that they understand what they were doing to us by dragging everything out so long. Glen wouldn't do that, and he didn't want me to do much either, so I spent my time being mad at Glen. Our marriage was full of stress. Many times it took several vigorous walks around the block together before we could even speak to each other.

We were both vulnerable, and our weaknesses began to reveal themselves. My need to talk began to bother Glen. He didn't want to hear all about my difficult days because his days were difficult, too. My up-and-down moods turned into all down ones, and I cried frequently.

The insurance situation and the manslaughter trial together wore me down, and I didn't want to reason—I wanted to fight. Glen didn't look like a peacemaker to me anymore; he looked like Mr. Milquetoast. I wanted him to protect me from the cold, cruel world and make people be nice to me. Instead, he kept telling me I should be patient with the insurance company and with the court system. The more I nagged him to get involved, the more uninvolved he became.

That fall I attended a seminar led by Florence Littauer where she talked about the different temperaments of people, and she gave each person a temperament test. After I discovered what my temperament was, I went home and had Glen take the same test. Then I began to understand why we were having difficulty. Our temperaments were opposite, which is typical of most couples. Most of the time that's wonderful because you and your partner each have strengths where the other has weaknesses, and you can build each other up.

If you're a serious person, it's nice to have someone who is fun, can tell jokes, and sees the funny side of life. But those same things that are fun and mesh you together when everything is going right also tend to pull you apart when you're going through tragedy. I believe, as married couples, we often don't understand each other and so we do not recognize our partner's needs. Those needs are built into our temperaments.

There are four basic temperaments: Sanguine, Choleric, Melancholy, and Phlegmatic. Glen's major temperament is Phlegmatic: "low-key personality, easy going and relaxed, calm, cool and collected, happily reconciled to life, an all-purpose person."[1] Some of the Phlegmatic's weaknesses are: "avoids responsibility, quiet will of iron, too compromising, resents being pushed, stays uninvolved, resists change."[2]

My temperament is a split of Choleric and Melancholy: "must correct wrongs, strong-willed and decisive, moves quickly to action, insists on production, idealistic, persistent and thorough, sees the problems."[3] Some of a Choleric/Melancholy's weaknesses are: "impatient, demanding of others, remembers the negatives, moody and depressed, self-centered, persecution complex, depressed over imperfections, hard to please, critical of others, dislikes those in opposition, unforgiving."[4]

No wonder we were having trouble! Our basic responses to adversity were so different. As I listened to Florence I began to realize that Glen was not responding differently from me just to buck me, and he wasn't necessarily saying I was wrong. We simply were looking at the world through different eyes.

Each temperament is driven by different goals. The Sanguine wants to have fun; the Choleric wants to have control; the Melancholy wants to have it right; and the Phlegmatic wants to have peace. So Glen's goal was to have peace, "Don't rock the boat"; my goal was to have control and have everything right. When Nathan died, all of our goals were challenged. Glen recalls:

> Marilyn mentioned the manslaughter trial, which is a criminal operation run by the district attorney's office. In some countries of the world the victim has a voice in these cases, but the victim has no voice in our criminal justice system. Marilyn is Choleric/Melancholy. The Melancholy wants everything to be perfect and the Choleric wants to control things to make them just and fair and equitable.
>
> Now how do you control the criminal justice system? The Phlegmatic says, "Anybody in their right mind knows you cannot control the criminal justice system."
>
> Marilyn would say, "Why don't you call the district attorney and find out what's happening with the case?"
>
> My brain says, "Why would I want to do that? We'll find out what's happening with the case when the district attorney does something with it"…I learned how to call the district attorney. Marilyn learned how to, as gently as possible, prod me into calling the DA. She really did. You have to *gently* prod a Phlegmatic. If you sternly prod a Phlegmatic, he sets his heels in and says, "I will not do it," and I've done that many times.

It is important to take the time to recognize that others are different, and to give them the space to be different. Be creative and look for ways you can meet the other person's needs. It will pay off.

While I am talking basically about the husband and wife relationship, you can adopt these principles with your children and your friends as well. Our daughter, Mellyn, has a temperament much like her father's. She did not want me to cry; she wanted things to stay as normal as possible. She didn't need a lot of people around and often retreated to her apartment when our house became crowded with people. I needed lots of people around and became depressed when everyone left.

Since Mellyn didn't want me to cry, I made sure I didn't cry in front of her. One day when Mellyn was in our home, I was very depressed. Because I felt I couldn't cry in front of her, I went into my bedroom, called my friend Nancy, and told her I needed help. Nancy quickly came to the house and told Mellyn I had called her. When Mellyn came to the bedroom and found me sobbing, she was very hurt because I hadn't told her I was having a hard time.

We finally realized neither of us was wrong but we were grieving differently, and we needed to make room for each other. I began to understand that Mellyn missed Nate terribly even though she didn't show it in the same ways I did. Mellyn learned that each time I cried, I healed just a little bit more.

Our son Nathan was a strong Phlegmatic just like his father. I had learned to adjust to Glen, but when one of my children was so different from me, I had difficulty. As a Choleric mother I insisted each child make his or her bed every day, but Nate couldn't see any need in making his bed because after all, "I'll just get back into it tonight." I'm the type who wants to have everything done two weeks ahead of time, but Nate would say, "Why hurry to read the book? I have two days before I have to turn my book report in."

The summer before Nate died, he visited my parents in Michigan for several weeks. My mom told me that one morning she was busy in the kitchen preparing for company. Nathan was sitting in the family room enjoying his favorite Phlegmatic pastime...TV channel surfing. My mother sputtered, "Nate, how can you sit there and watch TV when Grandma is working so hard in the kitchen? You should be helping me."

Nate sauntered into the kitchen, leaned against the doorway, and quietly said, "Grandma, I'll do anything you ask me to do, but I'm volunteerin' for nothin'!" Now that's a phlegmatic's approach to life!

I wish now I had understood the temperaments when I was rearing my children. I've had to go to my remaining children and say, "I need to apologize to you for some of the ways I worked with you, because I just didn't understand."

Understanding our temperaments has helped all of us to realize what our normal, first reaction would be in a given situation. Now we are able to work on our deficiencies and emphasize our strengths without feeling the other person is disapproving of our behavior.

The Sanguine's basic underlying drive is to have FUN. If he loses his fun, he gets depressed. The Sanguine child can't sit very long in class, and he will have difficulty listening to a lecture unless the speaker is entertaining. Sanguines want to get involved, and when they enter a crowd, they see an audience to entertain. They have a childlike style of emotion even when they reach adulthood. Their emotions can be very short-lived and changeable. They cry hard but a few minutes later they can go on to something else.

Sanguines will come bouncing into a room and never know a stranger. They make wonderful waitresses, receptionists, salespeople, comedians, and talk show hosts. They talk easily to everyone. If others don't respond, they just keep on talking and don't even notice because they like to hear themselves talk. When they're angry, their anger generally doesn't last long. Once they have said everything they want to say, it's over and everything is fine. They can't understand what's wrong with all of those other people who are mad at them. When a Sanguine is grieving, he will try to forget his troubles by having fun. He will be one of the first to want to "get on with life." The Sanguine may tell jokes about the deceased, even at the funeral, and this will seem absolutely inappropriate to the sensitive Melancholy. Sanguines need constant encouragement and approval. You can keep a Sanguine going as long as you keep telling him he's doing a good job and keep recognizing his efforts. However, a

Sanguine will become depressed very quickly if the fun is taken out of his life.

The Choleric's major drive is for CONTROL. When Cholerics go through trauma, they try to deny the pain by becoming totally absorbed in their work, a hobby, or a social cause. They'll work furiously and may not want to come home for fear it will be too emotional and they might lose control. The one emotion Cholerics allow themselves is anger, and their anger is generally rooted in impatience because things aren't moving, people are slow, and they don't see any progress. They also may display anger when they're actually feeling sadness.[5]

It is almost impossible for Cholerics to say "I'm sorry," even if they feel it inside, because admitting blame makes them feel they're losing control and becoming vulnerable to other people.

Cholerics need to be appreciated for their responsible and dutiful endeavors. They need acknowledgment of their hard work. Some men come home after putting in many extra hours at work to hear their wives say, "I don't feel you love me anymore. I never see you. You don't seem concerned. You aren't involved with us."

The husband responds, "But I work sixty hours a week for you. What more do you want?" From the Choleric's point of view, he is showing love by the amount of work he produces, but it may not mean a thing to the wife who is home alone and needs to have some attention from her husband. It helps if we can understand how each temperament dictates our natural method of demonstrating love and concern for others.

The Choleric may react to grief by becoming engrossed or possibly even obsessed in his work or in a cause. The night Nathan died, I was overwhelmed with grief; however, my Choleric nature needed to take control of something. I needed to feel productive. By the time we got back to our home within an hour or so of Nate's death, I already had the funeral planned! Some people said, "Oh, she's holding up so well." I wasn't holding up well at all, but I saw a job that needed to be done, and I did it. That was my way of controlling an out-of-control situation.

Melancholies want PERFECTION. They want to be able to depend on how things are going to be; they're generally quite methodical. They have medium highs but very low lows. A melancholy trying to deal with grief may go into a severe depression and may withdraw deeply into himself. However, even in our deep depression, we manage to remember significant dates such as the day our child died, and we are sensitive to what people say and do. It is easy for us to remember how people hurt us by their apparent insensitivity to our situation.

When Melancholies are depressed, everybody knows it. Some of us get to the point where we don't talk at all. I didn't get that low, but I did have occasions when I felt a cloud of doom was over my head and I couldn't get away from it. At those times, having people around me who wanted to have fun was totally obnoxious to me. I couldn't understand those people because I felt so deeply about everything.

Phlegmatics have a great desire for PEACE, sometimes peace at any price. They fear conflict, and it is hard for them to express their feelings. Phlegmatics may show little emotion even when they are experiencing grief, and those around them may think they have already worked through it. In truth, it could be they have not handled it at all. It may take them several years to deal with their loss. They often respond to anger with sadness which is just the opposite of the Choleric, who usually responds to sadness with anger. When these two temperaments marry each other, and that frequently happens because opposites tend to marry, they are likely to have problems.

As a Choleric, when I'm sad about something, my sadness may come out in anger as it did when I was faced with the insurance problems. I wanted Glen to go tell the other families what this was doing to us. Why couldn't they understand? I was angry because I was hurting. Glen pulled back and wanted to be really quiet about it. His anger was portrayed in his deep sadness, and he wanted to keep peace.

I said to Glen, "You aren't protecting me. You aren't taking care of me and meeting my needs. What's wrong with you? I don't know you anymore." And I'm sure Glen felt the same about me.

Phlegmatics need a sense of value—they need to feel they're important. Because they have difficulty showing emotion or expressing their thoughts, they are often lost in the crowd and it's easy for people to assume they have no feelings or thoughts. The partner who sticks with them, though, will eventually find out what's going on in the Phlegmatic's mind.

Understanding the temperaments will help when you and your family are in a crisis. The death of a child may be the worst thing you ever face in your life, and differences in temperaments can increase the stress within the entire family. You need to remember that other family members loved that child as much as you did. Don't alienate them. Reach out to them. Pull them in so you can enjoy together the love and memories you shared and try to learn the underlying needs of each other. Recovering from grief can be a life-changing experience.

It is important that we give family members room to grieve in their own way, but we also need to work at keeping in touch with each other. At the lowest point in our relationship, Glen and I seldom spoke to each other. I used the TV as my protection and often chose to watch TV rather than have to talk to Glen. One night Glen got between me and the TV, looked me straight in the eye, and said, "I don't care what you do, but I'm not leaving!" In the emotional state I was in at that point, I can't say that was really good news! However, we did decide that night that we were willing to at least try to work on our marriage.

Some of the things Glen and I did were to talk to and listen to each other. I got the temperament test out and I said, "I know you don't like this kind of thing, but I need you to listen." As I read the characteristics of the Phlegmatic, I described Glen right down the line.

Glen said, "Let me see that."

Sure enough, this test had him pegged. I asked, "What do you want me to do for you? How can I help you?"

He said, "I need peace and quiet."

It was easy to spot our difficulty when I said, "I need to talk. I need to tell someone how I feel, why I get mad, upset, and frustrated every time this trial gets postponed. Yet I realize that when I talk to you it upsets you, and you feel helpless. I know you can't do anything about the justice system, but I still need to get it out."

Finally Glen said, "Well, when you get upset, why don't you call Joan or go see Nancy?" This was a concession for Glen because we always had the policy that we didn't talk about our personal problems outside of our family. He realized, though, that in this situation he was helpless. He couldn't do anything about it, and when he heard me complain he just got more depressed and felt more inadequate. He said, "You need to have someone you can talk to who won't feel the load like I feel it."

Once I aired my feelings with someone else, I could come home and love Glen. We began to understand it was all right to be different. Just because I was doing something my way didn't mean the way Glen was doing it was wrong.

As we talked about Glen's needs, he tried to explain to me that when he went into the bedroom, closed the door, and just sat in the Lazyboy chair, everything was really OK. He just needed a little peace and quiet. He simply wanted to be left alone for a while.

This was hard for me to understand, because with my temperament, the only reason I would ever go into the bedroom and close the door was in the hopes that someone would come in and ask, "What's wrong?"

As we were listing our needs and desires, Glen said, "I need to know that you aren't disappointed in me, that you aren't angry with me or blaming me because this insurance situation isn't going better." I hadn't realized that when I let off steam about our situation I was pushing Glen deeper into a hole of guilt. I just knew I needed confirmation that he thought I was doing all right and that he still liked me.

We planned special times to be together. We drove to the mountains, walked around Lake Arrowhead and talked. Sometimes we just drove to a nearby regional park, ate dinner in our motor home, and talked. Where we were didn't matter, but talking did. We became reacquainted and slowly began to discover those special traits that had drawn us together originally.

I can now say after more than 47 years of marriage that we really are enjoying those differences again. Glen's sense of humor, for a while an irritant to me, is now wonderful—nice and dry. I appreciate his ability to be a peacemaker although right after Nate's death I didn't want peace. Glen does not enjoy traveling and speaking as much as I do, but he has given me room to do so because I love it. He is my support system, and even travels with me when he can.

People often ask me, "What does poor Glen do while you are traveling?"

Without even a twinge of guilt, I can now say, "He enjoys some peace and quiet!"

We back each other up now, but it has taken a great deal of effort and commitment to each other, to our marriage, and to God to get to this point. Be assured, it has been worth every bit of effort!

Since Glen retired, we have chosen to sell our house and travel full-time in a motor home. We love traveling together, and in those close quarters, it sure is good we like each other! We spend our summers at America's Keswick in New Jersey. God is using us; we are sharing our story together, and we're aware that God brings people to us who need to know that God cares and will meet their needs and heal their broken hearts.

Each of us can be a rose to the people in our families who are grieving differently than we are. Reach out to them and say, "It's OK that we're different; the most important thing is that we stick together. We need each other. We loved this person together. We need to share our hurt together." You can be a rose of uniqueness if you make room for those you love.

How thrilling to realize our precious Lord created each of us to grow in His garden as unique, priceless roses.

	Popular Sanguine	Powerful Choleric	Perfect Melancholy	Peaceful Phlegmatic
Clothing	Bright	Functional	Conservative	Casual
Voice	Loud	Decisive	Sensitive	Calming
Gestures	Grand	Strong	Confined	Relaxed
Work Style	Casual	Productive	Organized	Low-key
Speech	Busy	Commanding	Precise	Peaceful
Demeanor	Exciting	Intense	Reserved	Amiable
Posture	Rhythmic	Determined	Erect	Leisurely
Emotions	Erratic	Controlled	Deep	Concealed
Strongest Emotion	Joy	Anger, Denial	Sadness	Fear
Reaction to Grief	Tears, Need humor	Increased productivity	Depression, Sensitivity	Sadness, Introspection

Chart compiled by Marilyn Willett Heavilin from her own material and material presented in *Personality Puzzle* by Florence Littauer and Marita Littauer, published by Revell, 1992.[6]

The Rose of Tenderness

O Lord, don't hold back your tender
mercies from me! My only hope is in your
love and faithfulness. Otherwise I perish,
for problems far too big for me to solve are
piled higher than my head.

PSALM 40:11-12, TLB

*A*fter Nate's death, many people said to Glen and me, "You'll find this crisis will draw you closer together." Now, after many years of working through our differences, I believe we are closer, but that wasn't true at first. For many couples crisis pulls their families apart because it accentuates nearly every aspect of your marriage, weak or strong.

A salesman named Joe was trying to sell us a motor home, and in a talkative and friendly manner he asked about our family. We explained that we had two married children and then told him about Nate.

He started asking some very knowledgeable questions. "How have you dealt with the grief? Your marriage seems to be OK. How have you managed that?"

I said, "Joe, what's your story? I sense you have dealt with a major loss."

His eyes filled with tears as he recalled, "My second wife and I had been married just a few months. My son came to visit one weekend. He was riding his bike near our house when he was struck and killed by a drunk driver.

"He was my only son. When he died, everything in my life changed. For the next year I spent all of my time following the manslaughter trial. Nothing else mattered. The driver was given a light sentence which didn't satisfy me, and I was consumed with anger.

"My new wife didn't know my son well, and she couldn't relate to my grief. Soon, we stopped talking to each other. I stayed away from home as much as I could. I blamed myself— why did I let him ride on that busy street? I should have gone with him.

"I became more and more depressed. Our marriage ended within a year."

Joe looked wistfully at Glen and me and said, "If you can survive the death of three sons, you've got something pretty special!"

Joe was right. Any couple whose marriage weathers a crisis as severe as the death of a child is in the minority today. We do need to realize that in the face of severe trauma, the possibility of at least emotional separation from our partner is very real. You don't have to become a statistic if you're willing to work at keeping your marriage together. Let's look at some factors which tend to break up a marriage.

GUILT. It is natural for a person to experience guilt, deserved or undeserved, when a loved one dies, but it is destructive when the guilt is allowed to fester and grow out of proportion. We need to talk to someone openly about our feelings.

When Nate died, one of my first thoughts was, *Why didn't I go to the game with him? This wouldn't have happened if I had been there.*

By the time I told Glen how I felt, I had built a strong case against myself. In an effort to help me analyze my feelings, Glen said, "Why didn't you go to the game?"

"Well, I had been to one on Tuesday and I was going to the one on Friday. Also, I would have had to drive to Hemet alone, fifty miles away, at night, and I'd never done that before."

Glen very logically said, "So even if you had gone, you probably would not have been in the same car with Nate."

"Well, probably not," I admitted.

Glen continued, "If you had been in the car with Nate, how could you have prevented the crash?"

"I don't know, but mothers are supposed to be able to protect their children!" I sobbed.

In a very loving and yet logical way, Glen helped me see how unwarranted my guilt was. Whether your guilt is perceived or real, it must be faced and dealt with, or it will become a germ that will invade your wound and fester until it controls and infects everything in your life.

BLAME. Although it may not be justified, couples often build a case of blame against each other. A husband may think, *If she hadn't let him play in the front yard, he wouldn't have been able to run out into the street,* even though they had both allowed the child to play in the front yard on previous occasions. Whether or not the husband is justified in blaming his wife, these feelings must be carefully and sensitively exposed, discussed, and eliminated, or a wedge will start to form between them.

LACK OF COMMUNICATION. Often a wife will tell me, "He never talks anymore. I don't know what he's thinking. He eats and sleeps at our house, but that's it. We're strangers." A spouse's grief may be so all-consuming that he can't risk talking about it for fear of losing control. Getting this person to open up will take a lot of tender, patient probing.

NOT UNDERSTANDING SEXUAL NEEDS. When Laura and Jim's daughter died, they were both overwhelmed with grief, but they responded differently. Within a few days after their daughter's death, Jim wanted to have sexual relations with Laura; he needed that emotional release and the assurance that she still cared for him. Laura was indignant. "How can you think about enjoying yourself like that when we just buried our daughter?"

Couples who have lost little children may have opposing responses also. I heard one young father say, "I think we should have another baby right away." His wife responded, "I'm afraid of getting pregnant. I don't ever want to love anyone that much again."

These are all normal responses, but they can cause difficulty if they are not discussed and resolved. A wife who is afraid of being sexually intimate will still usually enjoy being held and tenderly cared for. Be sensitive to each other's needs, concerns, and fears. Give each other time to work through the feelings.

EXPECTING TOO MUCH OF OURSELVES. I am quite melancholic in my temperament and am very much the martyr, so it takes me a long time to admit I've had enough. One evening in May, after Nate had died in February, I reached a point of total desperation. I sobbed, "I can't ever go back to school. I have to get out of here."

Glen could have just given me a pep talk saying something like, "You're a big girl now. You need to get ahold of yourself and get on with life."

Instead he chose to show me the tenderness I needed, and very calmly said, "Where do you want to go?"

I really didn't care, but the first place that popped into my mind was Hawaii. That was a Thursday evening; we left on Sunday! I'm sure the travel agent wondered about us. She asked, "Which islands do you wish to visit?"

Glen and I shrugged our shoulders and he said, "We don't care. You decide."

"What hotel would you like to stay at?"

"We don't care. You decide."

We really didn't care. We knew we had to get away, but the place or the hotel simply didn't matter. Nothing mattered right then except that our son was dead and we were hurting.

With mixed emotions, I said goodbye to my remaining two children on Mother's Day morning—I felt a twinge of guilt because I was leaving them, but I knew we had to do this. Was I running away? Perhaps—but I decided it was all right. Even Jesus had to get away from the crowds once in a while.

I wrote in my journal:

Today is the day we fly to Hawaii! I still can hardly believe it, but I am getting excited. That excitement is mixed with twinges of remorse and guilt. Remorse because of why we need this trip, and guilt because we're trying to enjoy ourselves so soon after Nate's death and because I've never been away from my kids on Mother's Day. I felt funny leaving them.

Today I have been able to handle the verse about "forgetting the things that are behind." I believe I am beginning to desire that, but until now, that verse just made me angry. I have been fighting against that idea, so I know this desire to "forge ahead" has to be from the Lord. It surely didn't come from me. Perhaps a new day is dawning—one in which we can build a future with new memories and let the old memories rest. I hope so.

The next day:

I awoke this morning with the same old thought, *Nate is gone.* But it didn't hit me like a kick in the stomach; it was more like a "nagging backache." It's always there, but I'm learning to live with it.

The trip to Hawaii was good for us; it was our first extended vacation without the children in twenty-four years. The trip helped us begin to build some memories which didn't include Nate and it gave us a temporary release from the pressures at home. Since that time, Glen and I have traveled to Japan, England, Bermuda, and Australia, and we made a return trip to Hawaii. Those trips took effort on our part. Most of the time it would have been easier to stay home and wallow in our misery. I didn't enjoy tending to all of the details traveling requires, and it was hard to move out into a new environment, but it did help.

Now we don't wait for the pressure to build up so high. We take small trips often, and our marriage has become stronger because we have spent time alone with each other away from all of the reminders and problems.

LACK OF SPECIAL ATTENTION. In the face of the personal and family tragedy that we were dealing with, I needed a way to communicate to Glen that he was important to me. Nathan was important and his death was important, but Glen needed to feel that in spite of all that was happening around him, he was important, too.

After some of the dust had settled, I said, "Glen, I want you to choose a day and take off work. In fact it would be even better if you took a day and a half."

"Why?"

"I'll tell you later."

When the day came, I gave Glen a list of instructions. "Get in the car. Back out of the driveway. Drive down Cajon Avenue. Turn left at the next traffic signal...." We followed this little sequence of clues and ended up at a Victorian mansion which was a bed-and-breakfast inn. In the trunk of our car nestled a wicker picnic basket with a chilled bottle of sparkling cider, cookies, cheese, fresh fruit, and a tape recorder with a cassette tape of "Music for Lovers," and Glen would be very quick to add, "And she brought a black nightgown!" We spent the evening in a Victorian mansion with a player grand piano which Glen loved, and I had the opportunity to show Glen some tenderness and say, "In spite of all we're going through, you're important to me. You are a very important person."

PERSONAL RESPONSES TO GRIEF. Several years ago, Glen and I led a workshop on "How We All Grieve Differently" for the National Conference of The Compassionate Friends in Omaha, Nebraska. When we finished, Nancy, one of the conferees, stood and gave a beautiful example of how she found a way to meet her husband's needs even though they were grieving differently and he seemed unable to express his feelings to her.

Before our son was killed my husband and I had a good marriage. Even though we've had lots of tragedy, we always managed to get through everything. But after our son died, my husband just clammed up. He didn't want to have anything to do with me; he didn't talk. He just went to work, went to the cemetery, came home, and that was it. This went on for two years.

I felt completely abandoned. I had six other kids, and they looked to me for emotional help; but when it came to me, I was on my own. This was the worst time to be on my own. I didn't understand him. I began to resent the fact that my husband wasn't there for me as he had always been when we went through so many other things.

Finally, I don't know why I thought of it, but I got a notebook and I started to write to him in the notebook. I left it in his underwear drawer where he would have to see it. I wrote about all sorts of things, things I was feeling, things I knew he was feeling. I wrote about how good he was all through our marriage when different things happened and told him what a great guy he was. I told him I didn't know what had happened, but I felt I didn't have him anymore.

He always read my notes, but he never said a word. After a whole year of me writing in the notebook and sticking it in his drawer, he finally came out of his shell. It was almost three years after our son's death, and now our marriage is better than it has ever been. Having a good relationship with him again is worth all of the effort I put forth.

Even though they were grieving differently, and her husband had isolated himself, Nancy found a way to extend loving tenderness to him.

In an article on coping with heartbreak, Robert Veninga states:

> When a husband and wife share a heartbreak, each must plot his or her own defense. You cannot plan the defense strategies of your partner nor can you plot a joint defense, for a heartbreak really is a solitary experience.[1]

In many ways grief is a solitary experience, but you can be a rose of tenderness as you make the effort to tell your spouse how you feel and what your needs are, and likewise try to learn what your spouse's needs are. We are extremely fragile people at this point, but we will become stronger as we spread the fragrance of our roses around us and we realize what is important to us. Don't let go of those loved ones you have. Don't let the differences part you. Bring yourselves together. Keep looking for the roses. They're there.

The Rose of Love

> But God showed his great love for us
> by sending Christ to die for
> us while we were still sinners.
> ROMANS 5:8, TLB

*I*n the self-help support group, The Compassionate Friends, we often hear, "If it works for you, you can share it." This chapter is written on that premise. While it is my hope that this book will be of help to all bereaved people from all situations and all beliefs, I am a Christian and I look at life from the Christian perspective. Therefore, to me, this chapter is crucial.

It is my prayer that this book will be helpful to all who read it whether they know Jesus as their personal Savior or not, but it is also important for me to state the reason I have been able to accept Jimmy, Ethan, and Nathan's deaths. I believe it is primarily because of the source of strength available to me through Jesus Christ, the Rose of Love.

Without the Rose of Love there would be no book because I would have no hope. The Rose of Love is my best Friend, my Comforter, and my Redeemer. He is revealed in the Bible as God, Jesus Christ, and the Holy Spirit.

If you have not met Jesus Christ before, please let me tell you about Him. Jesus became my Redeemer when I realized, at a very early age, that in my own power I would not be able to go to heaven when I died. I recognized I could not remove the sin which was in my life and I needed help. My mother explained that Jesus Christ loved me and He had died for me as a sacrifice for my sins even before I was born. At that moment I invited Jesus Christ into my life and He became my Savior.

Through the years, as I have learned more about God and as He has let me see how much He loves me and cares for me, He has become my best Friend. He never criticizes me; He always listens when I need to talk; He is constantly looking out for my best interests.

The Bible refers to Him as the God of all comfort: "Blessed be God, even the Father of our Lord Jesus Christ, the Father of mercies, and the God of all comfort; who comforteth us in all our tribulation, that we may be able to comfort them which are in any trouble, by the comfort wherewith we ourselves are comforted of God" (2 Corinthians 1:3-4).

As I have experienced the deaths of three of my sons, God has become my Comforter. He is always available to me; He is not impatient with me; He doesn't judge me or rebuke me for admitting I hurt. God has experienced sorrow. He, in fact, was a bereaved parent, because He, too, had a Son who suffered and died. But the exciting news is God's Son didn't stay dead. He conquered death for each of us so that we can have the hope of spending eternity with Him in heaven. We also can have the hope of seeing our loved ones again.

I have vivid memories of a special night when Nate was five years old. I was tucking him into bed and he seemed restless and unable to settle down. I asked him if there was a problem. He squirmed a little and then said, "I'm not sure I've invited Jesus into my heart."

I asked him why he wanted to invite Jesus into his life. "Because I've done some wrong things, and I want to make sure I'll go to heaven."

I listened as Nathan prayed and asked Jesus to come into his heart and live with him. After that there was no doubt in Nate's mind. He referred to the event often. As he grew, we saw the effect of the decision in his desire to study God's Word and in his submissive attitude toward us and toward God. How thankful I am I can look back on that evening and have confidence I will see Nate again.

"And now, dear brothers, I want you to know what happens to a Christian when he dies so that when it happens, you will not be full of sorrow, as those are who have no hope. For since we believe that Jesus died and then came back to life again, we can also believe that when Jesus returns, God will bring back with him all the Christians who have died" (1 Thessalonians 4:13-14, TLB).

Jesus understands my sorrow. He experienced abuse, rejection, and death. He wept when others were grieving. He felt their sorrow and He feels my sorrow and yours. Jesus comforts us so we can comfort others. He wants us to pass it on.

When Jesus left this earth, He promised that the Holy Spirit would come to dwell in all Christians: "And I will pray the Father, and he shall give you another Comforter, that he may abide with you for ever" (John 14:16).

When I first became a Christian, I did not understand the ministry of the Holy Spirit in my life. However, in my late twenties I met a group of people who talked about the Holy Spirit as though He were a real person! Through a Bible study with that group I discovered that the Holy Spirit dwells in me and His purpose in my life is to convict and convince of sin, but He is also with me to comfort me. He sees my needs even before I do and He asks God the Father to meet my needs.

Those days when I was so discouraged and couldn't reach out for help, the Holy Spirit would know my needs and would plant the thought in a friend's mind, "Call Marilyn; she needs you today."

The Holy Spirit is the one who convicts me when I harbor unforgiving attitudes toward others. He also gave Glen and me the desire and ability to rebuild our marriage relationship.

God, in the person of the Holy Spirit, comforts my heart, assures me I will see my children again, and gives me the power to live my life as a victor rather than a victim.

If you do not know Jesus, I encourage you to invite Him into your life now. Jesus has extended the invitation to you:

"Come unto me, all ye that labour and are heavy laden, and I will give you rest" (Matthew 11:28).

Some of you may not want to deal with this right now. Perhaps you have "put God on hold." You may be asking a lot of questions: How could a God of love let my child suffer and die? or, Why my child? I talked with one bereaved parent who recalled, "At first I asked why, and then the question came back, Why not? Who am I to say my family should be exempt from trouble? Am I really more deserving of a trouble-free life than my neighbor or my friend?"

I cannot solve all of life's complex problems, and I, like you, certainly have asked why and haven't come up with profound answers. But I do know God loved each of us enough to offer His only Son as the perfect and permanent sacrifice so that you and I might have eternal life.

The same God who loved Glen and me enough to provide a sacrifice for our sins also allowed some people we loved dearly to die sooner than we thought they should. I can't explain God or God's ways, but I am confident enough of His love for me, and for Jimmy, Ethan, and Nathan, to say, "I trust Him, and you can trust Him, too."

On several occasions I have presented a workshop for bereaved people entitled, "My Faith: A Help or a Hassle?" I try to be very honest in that session as I share that many times I stumbled over what other Christians said I should believe or what they thought the Bible taught. I had several alternatives, two of which were to believe the people and be totally disillusioned about Christianity, or to study Scripture for myself and find out what the Bible really taught pertaining to suffering and grief.

I chose to study Scripture and get the facts straight from the source. As I did, I discovered that Christ Himself grieved as He looked over Jerusalem and said, "O Jerusalem, Jerusalem...how often would I have gathered thy children together, as a hen doth gather her brood under her wings, and ye would not!" (Luke 13:34). It is obvious that His heart was breaking over what could have been. We also see, when Mary and Martha grieved over the death of their brother, Lazarus, that while Jesus reminded them of the hope of the resurrection, He did not rebuke them for weeping. In fact in John 11:35 it states simply, "Jesus wept."

I see through Scripture that Jesus is very compassionate and He has promised to draw nigh to the brokenhearted (Psalm 34:18). I learned a long time ago not to blame Christ for what His sometimes poorly behaved children do.

If you are experiencing grief, I'm sure you have many questions. You probably feel heavy laden, and you undoubtedly wish you could cast your burdens on someone else so that you could rest. I urge you right now to talk with Jesus and tell Him this is the heaviest burden you have ever had to bear. You are grieving because of a great loss and you are so very tired. Hand Him your burden and ask Him to carry it for you.

Jesus is the most beautiful rose of all. Take a deep breath of the fragrance of His love and compassion, and then perhaps you can share His fragrance by reaching out to others who are hurting, too.

Let Jesus, the Rose of Love, stand in the center of your bouquet of December roses.

The Rose of Farewells

> In just a little while I will be gone
> from the world, but I will still be present
> with you. For I will live
> again—and you will too.
>
> JOHN 14:19, TLB

So often as I talk with bereaved people, they lament, "But I didn't get to say goodbye." When there is no farewell, we tend to feel cheated. Is this just a modern-day, American expectation? I don't think so. As we look through Scripture, we see that farewells are very important. The Old Testament records a ritual of farewell that included a blessing to the remaining family, a benediction on the past, and a promise for the future. It gave the dying family member the opportunity to bless his family, and it gave the remaining family the chance to affirm their love and respect for the dying person.

In the New Testament, we find that Christ spent a great deal of time offering farewells to His disciples. He prepared them for what was to come; He assured them that He cared about them; and He gave them instructions for the future. Even from the cross He asked John to take care of His mother, Mary. His disciples watched as Christ died; they cared for His body, they visited the tomb, and they openly grieved.

The night Nathan was killed by the drunk driver, our family rushed to the hospital feeling the enormous need to see our boy, but we were put on hold. We were asked to fill out insurance forms, give information about our car and about Nathan, but we were given very little information in return. Finally we saw nurses rushing a gurney across the hall and into a waiting elevator. As the body was whisked out of our sight, we realized it was Nate. We did not recognize we had just seen our son alive for the last time. Soon a nurse came to tell us Nathan had died while they were trying to prepare him for surgery.

A short time later we walked out of the hospital surrounded by friends and family. We all gathered at our house in the wee hours of the morning to plan a funeral for our beloved son. During the next few days we did all of the things we were told to do....make phone calls, see the people, prepare Nate's funeral clothing, choose a casket, choose a burial plot, plan a service, attend the funeral.

A few days after the funeral, the numbness of grief began to wear off just a little. I was driving down the freeway in my autopilot mode when the fog lifted for a brief moment, and it hit me. *We didn't get to see him at the hospital. We didn't get to gather as a family around his form and pray. WE DIDN'T GET TO SAY GOODBYE THE NIGHT HE DIED!*

Then the questions and emotions started pouring into my consciousness. *Why didn't they let us see him at the hospital? They didn't even ask if we wanted to see him. I'm his mother! I should have been able to hold him one last time. Who did they think they were that they could make those decisions for me?*

Then my feelings of frustration turned to God. *I'm trying to trust You. I believe You were in control of the situation the night Nathan died...but then...why didn't You arrange for us to see him? Why didn't we get to say goodbye? I NEEDED TO SAY GOODBYE!*

A few nights later, I awoke from a sound sleep. I sat up in bed, and I saw Nathan standing at the end of my bed. He was wearing the clothes he wore the night he died. He had his gym bag in one hand. As I reached out to him, he stepped back. He gave me his beautiful smile; he waved goodbye, and he was gone.

I sat on the edge of the bed for a few moments, not wanting to move or speak. When I did lie down, I drifted off into the most peaceful sleep I had had in weeks. God had allowed me to say goodbye to my precious son, and now I could sleep.

Years ago, when *Roses in December* was first published, I had wanted to include the above story, but the editor advised against it. He felt the reader would feel very uncomfortable with such a "mystical" story in a Christian book, so I left it out, although I did include it in one of my later books. Since that time I have talked with hundreds of bereaved parents both Christian and non-Christian, and I have heard scores of stories similar to mine. In my opinion, it seems that God understands the need for closure and for those final goodbyes even more than we mortals do. I do not believe that Christians need to seek out mystics or psychics to get answers and properly resolve their grief. God cares about His grieving children, and He alone will meet their needs.

Humans have an innate need for closure, the opportunity for that final farewell. I remember several years ago as we all watched the world grieve over the tragic death of Diana, Princess of Wales. I couldn't help but compare her tragic death to the death of President John F. Kennedy in 1963. I was pregnant with Jimmy at that time. Most of America, and I suppose much of the world, sat in front of TV sets watching what was happening in Dallas and then in Washington, D.C. However, few of us became active participants. Now, forty some years later, we have learned not to fear expressing our grief. We no longer just watch, we become involved. Millions of people gathered in London to say farewell to their Princess, while millions around the world found some way to say their own goodbye whether it be through signing an official book of condolence, attending a memorial service, sending a letter, or writing a message to the royal family by way of the Internet.

Recently, I looked through a collection of *Life* and *Look* magazines that my father left me from the Kennedy era. The magazines praise Mrs. Kennedy for being so strong and not showing emotion in public, although we have since realized stoicism is not always the best reaction to tragedy. When Princess Diana died, billions waited to hear Queen Elizabeth speak, and we hoped we would see some emotion. Are we being maudlin or unkind? I don't think so. We were looking to her to give us permission to grieve; we wanted to see her join with us in that universal emotion. Grief must be acknowledged before a proper farewell can be offered, and an appropriate farewell can move us toward healing.

On March 20, 1995, my husband and I were driving into the Indianapolis airport. We were returning home from a ten-day trip. My mom had open heart surgery ten days before I left on my speaking tour. I called each day to check on her and felt the need to check my cellular phone voice mail just one more time before we went into the airport. There was one message and it said, "Call Braswell's Nursing Home immediately."

My first thought was *My mother is dead!* But then, at the airport, as I nervously dialed the number, I reasoned, *But she was fine last night. They probably just need some insurance information. Don't panic.* However, by the time the third person at the facility had put me on hold without offering any information, I knew in my heart why they were trying to reach me. My father finally came to the phone, and I heard him say, "Marilyn, Mom is gone!"

My body quickly shifted into what our family calls "grief mode": In a sort of fog, almost like a robot, I automatically began doing all the things that need to be done when someone dies. An airport chaplain took us into his office, made phone calls for us, gave us coffee, prayed with us, and made sure we got on the right plane.

During our five hours in the air, I made multiple calls via airphone to our son, Matthew, who was helping my father walk through those early hours of grief. I had learned much about how I needed to deal with grief since Nathan's death twelve years earlier, so during one of the calls to Matt, I said, "Matt, please tell the funeral director I must see my mom tonight. I can't wait until she is in the casket. I have to see her as soon as I get home."

Matt understood my need, so he went to the funeral home with my request. When Matt realized the people there didn't understand the urgency of my request, he showed them a copy of *Roses in December*. Then he said, "The lady who wrote this book is the one who is requesting she see her mother tonight!" Well, bless Matt's heart! His tactics worked, and when I came in that evening, Matt, my dad, our minister and his wife, and several of the men from the funeral home were waiting for us at the mortuary. They had placed my mother's body on a draped gurney. She had a hospital gown on and a soft blanket was draped over her body. In the quiet and privacy of that moment, I got to tell my mom how much I loved her, how much I was going to miss her, and then I was able to kiss her and say goodbye. Once I had given my mother an appropriate, personal farewell, I could go on and tend to the details of the events that lay ahead of me

Just eighteen months later, September 7, 1996, I stood outside a room in the Intensive Care Unit of Redlands Community Hospital, and the doctor was explaining to me that my father was dying. I asked him how much longer my father had. The doctor said they were trying desperately to get the internal bleeding stopped, but death was imminent and could be just minutes or no more than hours away. I explained that while I understood it was awkward for the staff to have family in the room when they were working on my father, yet it was imperative that I be present when my father died.

I had not met this physician until earlier that day, but I quickly explained to him what I do for a profession. I also emphasized that my father still belonged to us and not to the hospital or its staff, and that we would have the final say in all decisions regarding his care. Apparently, I got my point across. In a little while the doctor came out and said, "All of you who want to be in the room when he dies should come in now."

Our minister, one of the ministers from my father's church, many of my dad's friends, Glen and I, and Matt and his wife, Debbie, and their three children, all gathered around my dad's bed. My son, Matt, put his mouth close to Grandpa's ear and said, "Grandpa, we're all here. You've done a good job. We've all turned out okay. We love you. You can go now."

Matt also commented, "According to Scripture, there are angels in this room, so we'd better be looking around!"

Matt held one of my father's hands and I held the other. I kissed my dad on the forehead and whispered, "I love you, Daddy." The great-grandchildren touched Grandpa's hand and said goodbye. Our daughter-in-law Debbie sang softly "There's a Sweet, Sweet Spirit in This Place."

The doctor, who was keeping his eye on the heart monitor, touched my hand and said, "It won't be long now." As the tears streamed down our faces, we stood silently as my father slipped into eternity. Our pastor prayed a beautiful prayer, committing this child of God into his Father's hands.

The next day I sat in the same office at the mortuary where I sat with my father eighteen months before when we had arranged for my mother's funeral. The funeral director, Ernie Marsteller, and I were great friends now. He remembered my request when my mom died, so he quickly said, "Marilyn, we have your father ready so that you can see him now." Ernie was quite surprised when I responded, "I don't need to see him now, Ernie. I was with him when he died. I've already said goodbye." This time I was finally able to do it right, and I could begin to heal.

Goodbyes are oh so difficult, and yet so very necessary. Goodbyes close a chapter for us. Goodbyes give us the opportunity to whisper anything that has been left unsaid. In some cases, perhaps when a person has died completely unexpectedly, goodbyes give us the chance to regain control of the situation. Goodbyes bring resolution, and they are vital to the healing process.

If closure is still needed, it is possible to achieve it even years after the death of a loved one. On the front page of our local newspaper recently was the headline "A mystery solved," along with the following statement: "A grandson's four-year search turns up the remains of Redlands' former fire chief, listed as missing since 1937 and buried as an 'Unknown White Man' in an Orange County cemetery."[1]

"This Sunday, exactly 60 years to the day after his disappearance, Horace Green will have his family at his graveside, where he has lain for six decades in a grave marked 'Unknown White Man.'"[2]

"This Sunday, however, Horace Green will be laid to rest by his family. And some fellow Redlands firefighters will be there with a new fire engine to honor the former chief, said current Fire Chief Mel Enslow...The VA has now installed an appropriate headstone on the old chief's final resting place. The VA also has provided an American flag, which at the memorial service Neil Anderson will present to his mother, the only one of Horace and Sarah Green's three children still surviving."[3]

Apparently Horace Green walked out of the VA hospital in 1937 and his family never heard from him again. While the actual cause of his death is still a mystery, the remaining family can at least say farewell to the loved one for whom they had been searching for sixty years! Closure can come at last!

When our seven-week-old Jimmy died of SIDS in the night, in 1964, it seemed that all the professionals thought their duty was to "protect" me. As the mortician took little Jimmy's body from his bedroom out to the funeral car, he told me to go into another room so that I wouldn't have to see my baby leave. He said that "would be best for me." I did what I was told to do...I went into the other room while they removed my baby from my home forever.

At the funeral home I was never really given an opportunity to sit alone with my baby. I touched his cold little hands, but I never dared to unwrap him. And the thought of being able to hold him just one more time never even entered my head. This chapter was never properly closed.

Just eighteen months later when we were told that Ethan, the smaller of our newborn twins was dying, we went to the hospital immediately, but we were not allowed in the nursery, nor were we allowed to touch our baby. We peered through the window and watched the doctors care for little Ethan. Occasionally the attending physician would come out into the hall and update us on what was happening. Ethan's condition worsened, and as he neared death, the nurses closed the drapes of the nursery window—to "protect" us, of course.

Through the next few days the professionals continued to "protect" me from anything that might not be pleasant, and once again I had no time alone with my little boy. To add to my already excruciating pain, I later discovered the hospital had sent everything that belonged to Ethan, including his arm band and his Christmas stocking, on to the funeral home. Without asking me or consulting with me in any way, the funeral home had discarded all of Ethan's belongings, including his armband and the Christmas stocking. I had nothing tangible, nothing to hold in my hand, nothing to put in a scrapbook, nothing to even show there actually was a little boy named Ethan Thomas Heavilin. One more time, I was not allowed to control how I said farewell to my child.

Glen and I lived in Indiana at the time of the boys' deaths, but my parents offered for the boys to be buried on the plots in Michigan where my parents planned to be buried. The plots were called "pillow plots." By the time Ethan died, we knew we were moving to California, so it was a comfort to think my parents were close enough to the graves to tend to them and take flowers to them. My parents figured they would live the rest of their lives in Michigan, so this arrangement made sense to us.

However, after Nathan died, my parents moved to California to be close to me and their remaining grandchildren. My father then requested that he and my mother be buried near Nathan. And when they died in 1995 and 1996, we honored their request. It has been a great comfort to me to have my parents buried in California, right near Nathan, but that left my babies "alone" in Michigan.

One evening I was talking with my funeral director friend Ernie Marsteller and one of his associates, Mike McIntire. During that conversation, they realized for the first time that Jimmy and Ethan were not buried here in California. I told them I had always dreamed of bringing those little boxes home to California, but I simply was overwhelmed with the process. Instantly these men said, "We will do that for you."

I gasped for breath and said, "You would really do that?" Then the tears came. I wanted this so badly, but I was afraid to even consider the possibility. I didn't want to get my hopes up. What if it couldn't work out? These men assured me that it was totally possible and they wanted to do it as a gift to me for all of the help I have given them. I still can't think of one thing I have done that could possibly warrant their generosity.

The plans were made and approved by the General Manager Rick Foster. Mike and Ernie flew back to Michigan to get our boys. They called me when the boxes had been disinterred. They called me the next day when they had a stopover in Atlanta. They called again when they arrived at the mortuary late Saturday evening, January 25. We went to the mortuary and I gazed at those little boxes...our boxes! The tears came in floods, but they were not so much tears of sadness...but tears of relief. Our boys were home at last!

Monday morning, I went back to the funeral home, and I sat in a room alone with those little boxes. I told my boys I loved them. I told them everything that has happened in the last 32 ½ years. I told them how much I loved them. I told them how grateful I was to have them so close to me after this time. I told them again how much I loved them. I put my hands on each of their caskets. I prayed over them. I kissed the lids of those caskets, and I said goodbye. Time alone with my boys...I had waited 32½ years for this. I needed no one to protect me or spare me. I needed time with my boys, and I got it! I was finally able to close these chapters of my life in a way that was comfortable for me.

Ah, farewells! They are so painful, but so necessary. If circumstances have not allowed you to say goodbye in a healing way, determine to do it now. Create a setting. Light a candle. Play some special music. Include others if you wish, or just quietly spend some time alone. Write in your journal, speak out loud, or just sit in silence. Allow yourself to pay honor to your loved one in a meaningful way. The rose of farewells is a rose that will set you on the path toward healing.

The Rose of Victory

> But despite all this, overwhelming
> victory is ours through Christ who loved
> us enough to die for us.
>
> ROMANS 8:37, TLB

*W*hen the police came to tell my friend Patsy her daughter Suzie had been in an accident, Patsy sensed it was very serious. Yet as she drove to the hospital, she reasoned, "Everything seems normal. Traffic is moving properly; people are walking down the street; the moon is shining; and the stars are still in the sky. If Suzie were dead, the whole world would stop. Everything would be in chaos—life could not proceed in its normal pattern."

However, when she arrived at the hospital, she discovered Suzie had died, and Patsy's world turned upside down even though the rest of the world did not stop.

I felt the same way after Nate died. I would watch people complacently shopping or enjoying a meal in a restaurant, and I wanted to shout, "How can you do that? Don't you know Nate is dead?"

When you're facing a severe crisis, your world does stop. Nothing else matters. Life loses its edge. The big question is, *Does the world ever start turning again?* You may wonder, *Will little things ever matter? Will I ever get excited about anything? Will I ever enjoy life to its fullest again?*

After Jimmy and Ethan died, we did eventually begin to enjoy life again. I got excited about Christmas for my children, and I did learn to enjoy long-awaited events. But once in a while I still cast a nostalgic look at what might have been.

Whenever I see twins, I wonder what it would have been like to raise Nathan and Ethan together. When I see a large family, I wish I could have raised all five of my children instead of just three. This year Jimmy would have been forty-one and his birthday was difficult for me. As I looked at other young men his age, I felt cheated because I didn't get to watch him grow up.

My heart cringes when I hear a mother yell angrily at her children or threaten to "give them away" if they don't behave. I'm tempted to reprove her and say, "You should appreciate your children and thank God you have them."

Our whole family really enjoyed Mellyn's wedding, but even Mellyn remembered the two brothers who were absent. The pillow which held the wedding rings was a satin one used to hold flowers at Ethan's funeral, and the flower girl carried a white wicker basket from Jimmy's funeral. Mellyn explained, "I want all of my brothers to be represented."

We did quite well at Matt's wedding a year and a half after Nate's death until we posed for a family picture. Then we didn't dare look at each other because we all knew what the others were thinking: *When we had the family picture taken at Mellyn's wedding, Nate was with us. He should be here now.*

As I watched many of Nate's classmates participate in Matt and Debbie's wedding, I wondered if Nate could see. Did he know his big brother married one of his best friends? Oh, how I wished I could talk with him!

Later, I watched Nate's friend Christian perform with his college glee club. I was thrilled for him, but my eyes filled with tears as I remembered when he and Nate had talked of attending college together.

Afterward, I told his mother how much I enjoyed the concert. Her response helped me a great deal. "I'm sure you enjoyed the program, but I know you must have been thinking what it would have been like to have Nate there because I was thinking about him, too." It feels so good to know others have not forgotten him.

Life is never the same after a loved one dies or you suffer some other major loss. But life can be good again—different, but good. As I look back over the past few years, I can mark turning points in my healing process: The first trip to Hawaii allowed me to step outside of my situation, removed me from some of the pressures, and gave Glen and me time to talk. Moving from full-time to part-time status at the school gave me freedom to spend more time at home and to visit with friends when I felt the need to talk. Leaving that position completely finally gave me room to discover some talents in writing and speaking that I didn't even know I had.

Another turning point came almost two years after Nate's death. I drove to the cemetery, sat on the grass near Nate's grave, spent some time thinking over the happenings since the accident, and then realized I was getting better. As I walked away, I knew I would not be coming again soon. For me, it was time to move ahead.

Making the decision to speak publicly about my experiences gave me a sense of new beginning and purpose, but it was not easy. Shortly after the funeral I received a card from a representative of MADD. I quickly put the card away and said, "I'll never get involved with any crusades."

Later, Florence Littauer invited me to speak at the HOPE Conference (Helping Other People Emotionally) in Anaheim, California. I worked hard, prepared my notes, and practiced my speech, but the evening prior to the conference I sat in Nate's room and sobbed for hours. I was certain I would break down in the middle of my talk.

Many of my friends attended HOPE, and I asked them to sit in the back of the auditorium so that I wouldn't be affected by their tears. They prayed fervently, and God gave me the strength to present my story without losing control. I was amazed at the response of the people; they said I had really helped them!

Shortly after that I was invited to attend the training for the MADD Speakers Bureau. I made it clear I was attending simply to gather information; however, to finish the course we were required to present a talk on drunk driving and send a tape of the speech to our trainer. I spoke to the student body at Nate's high school and was thrilled at the students' response. One of the girls in the audience asked me to speak to her youth group, and then someone else invited me to speak at a Kiwanis meeting. During the next six months I spoke forty-five times to all types of groups from Al-Anon to Kiwanis, to all of the driver's education classes in the San Bernardino City high schools.

A few years ago, I had the privilege of speaking in New Zealand. A woman native to New Zealand told me that while she and her husband were stationed in Germany, their five-year-old son was killed in an electrical accident. There they were, thousands of miles from their families, feeling very alone in their grief. An acquaintance gave them a German language version of *Roses in December.* This dear grieving mother was so hungry for help that she read the book, even though she had to translate much of it back into English. She shared that she felt as though my book was her only hope and it helped her in her time of need. One more reminder that our grief wasn't wasted.

Do stories like this make it worth losing my children? NO, but they help to make their lives and their deaths count. When I think of the other families who have lost a loved one and felt pain similar to mine, nearly 20,000 each year to drunk driving alone since Nate's death, I realize if I can persuade even one person not to drink and drive, if because Nate died, I can save even one family from this pain, or if I can help grieving parents pull their lives back together because Jimmy, Ethan, and Nathan died, I am establishing a living memorial to my boys. That's a rose!

Glen and I moved from San Bernardino to the town of Red-lands, California, three years after Nate's death. This town has been very healing for me. That first year, I walked and walked around the historic district. It is peaceful and quiet, and I found many memorials erected in honor of someone who had died.

One building is called "The Lincoln Shrine." The Shrine boasts the finest collection of Lincoln memorabilia west of the Rockies. The outside of the building features beautiful fountains and rose gardens. "In honor of Abraham Lincoln" is carved in stone around the top of the building; however, that is not the first thing I noticed. Over to one side is a small bronze plaque, dark with age, which reads: "In memory of Emory Ewart Watchorn." Emory was the only child of Mr. and Mrs. Watchorn and he died when he was in his early twenties. The shrine was built in 1931, and both Mr. and Mrs. Watchorn died many years ago, but even now as I stand and read that plaque, I feel a kinship with them. Mr. and Mrs. Watchorn survived their son by many years, but they did more than survive. They gave so that others like myself might be hopeful. Hopeful that we can be productive again even though we feel all motivation for productivity has died within us. Hopeful that through our actions our loved ones, like Emory Watchorn, will be remembered forever. To me, that is *Victory!*

Since the deaths of my three sons, I have had the dream deep inside me that somehow my boys would not be forgotten, somehow we would be able to do something to cause them to be remembered forever. But I also wanted to pass a legacy on to other bereaved people; a legacy of life after the death of a loved one. A promise of *Victory*.

In recent years I began to see the possibility that I might be able to do something in memory of my children that would out-last me. I shared my dream with my husband, and then we shared it with our pastor. I wanted to donate a statue to our church, one that would he especially appreciated by children. Our pastor introduced us to Linda Hundevadt Pew, a woman who works in bronze. I shared my dream with Linda. I am not an artist, so my "dream" was very sketchy. I wanted a statue that would depict how much God loves His children. That's about all I could give to Linda in the way of a description of what I wanted. However, Linda is a true artist and she was able to draw several possibilities for me. We chose Linda's concept of Christ holding a child and another child sitting at His feet.

On February 10, 1996, thirteen years after Nathan's death, the statue was completed. The next day, Glen and I went to "view" the completed statue for the first time. The tears flowed easily as we viewed this masterful piece of art. I was overcome. First with the thought that our plan was complete and it was beautiful. But then my mind wandered down through the pages of time when my descendants can come to see this work. A work that will outlast us. Then my thoughts moved to the bereaved parents who will see this work long after Glen and I are gone. They will see the bronze plaque that reads, "To the glory of God and in honor of all children, especially those who left too soon" and they will know…they will know this statue was erected for them and in honor of their loved one who left too soon. They will also know there is hope, hope of life after the death of a loved one; hope that they too can survive this horrible pain; hope that their loved one will never be forgotten. Now, that's *Victory!*

When my friend Diana's ten-year-old son Jimmy died in a shooting accident, Diana was devastated. She had lived in Phoenix only a few months and felt completely alone in her grief. After seeing a program about The Compassionate Friends on television, she called the headquarters to find out how to get in touch with a group in her area. She was disappointed to hear there was no chapter in Phoenix, but the national director gave her the name of another bereaved parent who had been trying to start a chapter and suggested Diana help her. Diana thought, "How can I do that? I can't help anybody else; I'm the one who needs help." But Diana did eventually become involved and was a founding member of the Phoenix chapter.

When she moved to Riverside, California, four years after her Jimmy's death, Diana started a new chapter of The Compassionate Friends. Since Jimmy's death, Diana has offered a listening ear and given hope to thousands of bereaved families. Through her support of other grieving parents, Diana has given purpose and meaning to Jimmy's life and to his death.

Jasmine was born with Down syndrome, but her parents praised the Lord because tests showed she did not have any heart defects. However, when little Jasmine was five and a half months old, the entire family contracted the flu. Jasmine became very ill and it was soon discovered that she did in fact have two holes in her heart. She died two weeks later of heart failure.

Her mother, Colleen, recalls, "At first I didn't see how I could help anybody else; I was just trying to help myself." Colleen met with a professional counselor regularly for several months and kept good notes on the counseling techniques which helped her the most. After she went back to her position as a childbirth educator, coworkers would call her when a client's child died, saying, "Since you've gone through this, I think you'll know just what to say." Now Colleen frequently counsels with bereaved parents of young infants. She states, "I'd rather have Jasmine back, but there are great rewards in sharing the pain of these parents. It's a memorial to Jasmine's life."

A newly bereaved parent said to me, "It bothers me to think I might become a better person, that I might benefit from my daughter's death. It doesn't seem anything good should come from a child dying."

I responded, "You have three choices. You could try to stay the same and not have her death affect you; you could give up on life and become a societal dropout; or you can become a stronger, more sensitive, wiser person because your child lived and died."

If you have lost someone you love, you will have to make a choice, too, but don't feel you must rush into any big decisions.

Do your grief work. Give yourself time. Seek God's heart, and let Him guide you into the unique purpose He has for you.

It may be months or even years before you realize you are actually enjoying the "ordinary" things of life again. I always enjoyed cooking and entertaining, but after Nate's death, cooking took too much energy and entertaining seemed purposeless. I am slowly learning to enjoy entertaining again, but it's on a different scale. Now I am more interested in what we do than in what we eat. For example, one Christmas I invited several of my neighbors to my home for dinner and then I took them all to watch Glen in a Christmas production. My purpose was to help them see the real meaning of Christmas—that Christ offers peace of heart. Therefore, I was comfortable planning a simple meal of store-bought lasagna, salad, and garlic bread. My meal was simple, but the program was very meaningful to each of them. Before Nate's death, I would have worn myself out cooking lots of special foods and would have been too tired to enjoy the evening's program. My priorities are different now.

Before Nate died, when the children were home, mealtime was always an event. We looked forward to being together and catching up on the news of the day. After Nate's death, Glen and I had difficulty eating at the dining room table when it was only the two of us. Nate's absence was just too obvious. We moved to another room to eat when we were alone. After three years, we moved into a different home, and then we finally were able to establish a pattern of eating in the dining room again.

There will come a day when I can enjoy watching a high school basketball game, and someday I will look forward to Christmas again. Eventually, when someone asks the simple question, "How many children do you have?" I will be able to answer without feeling my stomach churn.

A few years ago I attended the funeral of another young man who was killed by a drunk driver. I didn't want to go, but I felt I must offer my comfort to his wife and young child. While I was at their home, I met a woman whose children I had known, but I had not met Sandy before. I talked with her and openly shared our loss of Nate and how we were trusting God to get us through this experience.

After the funeral, Sandy came up to me and said, "I need to talk with you."

I said, "Fine, what about?"

Sandy responded, "I'm ready to take a step with God, and I think you can help me!"

That evening, over pie at a local restaurant, I was able to lead my new friend Sandy into a personal relationship with Christ.

Through her tears, she commented, "Nate may be gone, but his life lives on."

I know her statement is true. The evidences of Nathan's impact on the world are all around me. I see his influence on our friends, on his friends, and on our family. I know Glen and I are stronger people because of what we have faced in the years since Nate's death.

In 1996 Glen and I and our thirty-eight-year-old son, Matthew, were the keynote speakers for the opening session of the International Gathering of The Compassionate Friends in Philadelphia. We all shared honestly of the pain we have endured; we all spoke honestly of what helped and what didn't. But as I watched the video of that event, what I saw more than anything else was that we all LOVE each other, we are PROUD of each other, we are good FRIENDS, and we were able to give other hurting people HOPE. To me, that's *Victory!*

If our boys have the opportunity to look in on us from heaven, I hope they can say, "We may be gone, but our family is living on. They haven't given up. They are still serving God, and they are stronger people who are walking closer to God because of three boys who lived and died and are now living with God."

Friend, don't give up. As you go through this December of your life, God is willing to walk beside you. He understands when you have hard days; He understands you are grieving because of the terrible loss you've suffered.

Look around you and see the roses: the friend who is standing with you, the memories of your loved one, the Scripture God has given you, the kindnesses others have offered, the work God is doing in your heart. Gather those roses, and let their refreshing aroma fill your life with a confidence that Jesus hears and cares about you. Reach out to the Lord, and put your hand in His so He can lead you to VICTORY.

Keep looking for the roses!

When a Loved One Dies of AIDS

*M*y husband and I were sitting with other passengers and the crew of an airline, waiting for our delayed plane to arrive. Some of the passengers were reading newspapers that reported the death of alleged multiple murderer Andrew Cunanan. The country had been terrorized for days as the admitted homosexual had traveled across the country on a murderous rampage that had resulted in the death of five people, including the murder of designer Gianni Versace and ultimately Cunanan's own suicide. The comments from the waiting passengers ranged from "Well, he *was* a homosexual" to "I'm glad he's dead." I finally spoke up and said, "I'm relieved to know he's no longer a threat to the public, but I think we need to realize that regardless of what he was or what he did, today a mother is grieving because her son is dead."

After a pause, one of the airline stewards said, "May I speak to you privately?" He and I moved to a fairly private area, and he said, "I appreciated what you said about Andrew Cunanan's mother; now I have a question for you. If a son just found out that he is HIV positive, should he tell his mother?"

I asked, "Are you speaking of yourself?"

He said, "Yes."

"Does your mom know you are living a homosexual lifestyle?" I asked.

"Oh yes, she's known that for a long time," he replied.

"Then you obviously confide in her and you are probably close. I think you should show her you trust her and give her a chance to say or do everything she wants to say to you or do for you while she has a chance."

The handsome young man said, "Thank you so much for helping me. May I hug you?"

After we hugged, he thanked me again, saying, "I just didn't have anyone I could talk to, but I felt I could trust you."

I share this story to emphasize the point that a family grieves the loss of a loved one regardless of the cause of death. The means of death is not the issue.

We've become much more open in our dealings about HIV and AIDS, and yet we Christians still often let our biases and prejudices show. Regardless of what we believe about homosexuality, when a child dies, the parents and family need to be comforted and encouraged. These families should not be subjected to foolish and heartless comments. As Christians we have the opportunity to show the love of Christ to those who are hurting.

When someone is diagnosed with AIDS, each family member will experience his own individual response to the disease and to the patient. Often the family may not know a person is living a homosexual lifestyle until they find out he is an AIDS patient. Sometimes when homosexuals who have been alienated from their family discover they have AIDS, they return home hoping to restore their relationship and find someone to care for them during their final days.

Since AIDS is not part of my personal experience, I recently sent a questionnaire to several families who have lost a loved one to this tragic disease. Their responses are very revealing and can teach us much about the pain caused by AIDS. One sibling wrote, "I found out my brother had AIDS only four days before he died, so I didn't really have much time to mentally process what he was experiencing, nor did I have much time to actually talk with him about his feelings and whether he was saved."

The circumstances surrounding AIDS increase the normal stress a family experiences when someone is dying. Also, when a family member dies of AIDS, the family often feels ostracized from those who normally would support them in bereavement, and the family's needs may go unmet. Note this father's uncertain tone:

> We found out [the nature of our son's illness] approximately one year before he died. Honestly, we were very naive about HIV at that time. I just thought we could find a cure. It was more than a year after the first diagnosis that he suddenly became ill. Neither he nor we had advised his siblings. We told them only several days before he died. They were very supportive, and, of course, upset.

During the dying process and after a death, family members may experience many emotions such as anger, blame, and guilt, all directed toward the one who contracted AIDS as a result of his lifestyle. When someone contracts AIDS through a needed blood transfusion or through an accidental entry of the virus into the body, the family's anger may be directed toward a doctor, a hospital, or even the homosexual community.

These families all will need special understanding and patience from those around them. For proper emotional healing, they eventually will need to come to a point where they can forgive every person they see as involved in the problems and stigma that have been brought into the family. This includes the homosexual himself.

Regardless of how a person has contracted AIDS, he and his family need acceptance and support from those close to them.

We never told anyone for several years that our son died of AIDS, not even relatives. One doctor said it was like the plague in the Bible. He said God sent AIDS to rid the world of gay people. The funeral director said we could *not* have an open casket because the condition was contagious. The newspaper even called and stated they understood our son had died of AIDS. The fact that they knew put fear in us. We lived in fear. I wish we had known more about the disease and not been so fearful. Our son's death was at the beginning of the AIDS crises. Evidently everybody was scared and fearful. My wife was fearful of losing her job. We did not know what to do because of ignorance.

What is the responsibility of the Christian community in these cases? I have a Christian friend who is a nurse and has volunteered to care for patients with AIDS in the hospital where she works. When an elder from her church found out she works with AIDS patients, he commented, "Don't ever shake hands with me again!" How the Lord's heart must have ached when He heard that man's response.

We have some mending and catch-up healing to do in our Christian communities. Many of those who lost a loved one in the early years of the AIDS crisis are still bearing undeserved feelings of shame and guilt. They are still hiding their deep, deep pain. Today, most people are knowledgeable about how AIDS can be transmitted, but Christians sometimes seem to live in the dark ages and are not as informed as other members of our communities. Become knowledgeable about AIDS. Read everything you can and talk to those who are in the know concerning communicable diseases.

As Christians, we must also be caring. I'm not suggesting we should ignore the fact a family we are trying to help is dealing with a communicable disease, but the family's needs should take precedence over our fears we might "catch" AIDS. Jesus Christ set an example for us as He willingly interacted with lepers, prostitutes, and other social outcasts of His time.

A family who is caring for a patient with AIDS will need some physical help. Churches would do well to adopt such families. They could offer to care for the patient while the family gets some much needed rest, runs errands, or just gets away from the situation for a while. Church members could help care for the patient by bathing or feeding him, doing his laundry, or cleaning his room. They could relieve the family by spending time with the patient, reading and talking with him, taking him for a walk or a ride, or just listening to him share his thoughts, fears, and dreams.

We also can support the family members by listening when they want to talk about their suffering, anger, disappointment, fear, and possible feelings of guilt or blame. We can cry with the family, and after the patient dies, we can encourage the family to tell stories and share pictures and mementos of their loved one. We can find out what support groups in our community would be available to the AIDS patient and his family, and we can help put the family in touch with those agencies.

When a patient with AIDS has died, we should be sure to remember the family on the loved one's birthday, anniversaries, and holidays. Let them know how important that person was. Don't ever give them the feeling that because their loved one died of AIDS, he did not count. Make a special effort to bring the family into your home and associate with them in public. Sit with them in church and include them in activities.

Often when a homosexual child comes home with AIDS, he brings his partner with him or wants the partner to be allowed to visit him. Parents who have fought their child's lifestyle and have resented and perhaps even blamed the partner are going to feel immense anger. Make room for their anger; let them talk it out. Don't defend or argue—just listen. I have to be honest. If I were faced with that situation, I'm not sure how I would handle it, but I do know it would be very difficult for me to live in peace if my child was still alienated from the family when he died. We should help families to somehow make peace with a dying child so the child can die in peace and the family can live with themselves in peace after the child's death.

On the questionnaire I sent out, I asked the bereaved to tell me what others did that helped and didn't help and what they wished they knew before their loved one died. This is one father's response: "Our minister never came to see us. The chaplin at the hospital was our helper and rock. I wish we had known more about the disease and hadn't been so fearful." A sister shares this:

> My husband of only five months expected me to bounce back to being his full-time wife. He didn't support my need to be with my parents and younger brother, nor did he give me any room to grieve. Other friends loved me no matter how I acted or didn't act. They allowed me to grieve the way God made me to grieve. They always remembered my brother and weren't judgmental of me. They called, wrote notes, and weren't afraid to talk about my brother with me. I wish my brother would have told me he was a homosexual and that he had AIDS so that I could have had more of an opportunity to say "That's okay. I love you no matter what."...
>
> I wish I could have found a grief counselor or book that specialized in sibling loss to help me through the grief process. I also wish that I could have attended a grief camp somewhere for one or two weeks to concentrate on dealing with my brother's death rather than going home and having to just deal with it secretively since AIDS was so hush-hush then. I also wish my parents and younger brother could have attended the camp as well so we could all

understand what each other was feeling and what we could do to support each other.

What an opportunity we have to show Christ's love and compassion! We can reach out to our hurting brothers and sisters, or we can shun them and negate the opportunity Christ has given us to comfort others with the comfort we have received from Him. As Christians, we must never appear judgmental.

Oswald Chambers wrote that "to be able to explain suffering is the clearest indication of never having suffered."

My prayer is that we will use the comfort we have received from God in our time of need to comfort others who are hurting deeply.

When a Loved One Dies by Suicide

When someone dies, survivors often ask why. Why did he have to die so young? Why did she suffer so much? But when someone dies by suicide,* survivors are plagued even more with these unanswered questions and with feelings of anger and frustration toward the deceased person. I have not experienced this type of loss by suicide, so I sent out questionnaires to some families I knew who had. I'm grateful to them for their willingness to answer my questions so openly. One respondent, Mike, recalled his father's suicide:

> "Mike, Dad's dead! He hung himself!" That was the news I received from my brother as I returned home from my first semester of Bible college on December 20, 1990. Amid the shock and disbelief of this news, the reality was that my dad had committed suicide.

---

* In this chapter I have tried not to use the term "committed suicide," but rather have said, "died by suicide." Those who deal with survivors of suicide note that the terms "commit" or "committed" have often been interpreted as an accusation and are therefore offensive. The term "died by suicide" may seem bulky, but I am determined to avoid anything that would offend someone who is recently bereaved. Therefore, I have tried to absorb this new language into my thinking and conversations.

I had only been a believer for eight months, having trusted Christ as my Savior in an addiction recovery ministry where I was set free from 13 years of drug and alcohol addiction. News of my dad's death rocked my world! The only thing I could do was cry out, "Jesus, help me! Please, Jesus, help me!" as I sat in a chair, slumped over the kitchen table, and sobbed.

The remaining members of the family of a suicide victim are sometimes referred to (though not exactly accurately) as "survivors of suicide." In the following paragraphs, I'll highlight some of the issues that these survivors of suicide wrestle with, along with some of their answers to the questions I asked them. I'm also including some statements that appeared on the surveys, with little further comment from me.

As I read through the surveys, I became aware that one thought appeared on almost every questionnaire: "If God is a sovereign God and controls everything, why did He let this happen?" Here are some of the responses that described this struggle:

> I was very angry. I did not want to worship God after my son died by suicide. Since then I have somewhat "reconciled," but I still feel betrayed since I prayed that He would save my son.

> I was seriously angry at God when my son JD died. I have since built a new, deeper, more positive relationship with God.

> I believe in God; however, I felt I was being punished by losing three of my six children.

> I returned to school after Christmas break, and then it hit me. *God let this happen!* He allowed my dad to kill himself! What kind of God is this? I became angry and was on a mission to know more about this God who

let this happen to my family—to me. Keep in mind, I was a new Christian. I only became born again eight months prior to this. I remember praying, "Why should I serve You when You allowed this? I gave You my life at the Colony of Mercy, and You go and do this!"

I now realize how prideful that prayer was—I didn't give God anything He had not already given me. His sovereign control over my life and the affairs of the world do not take Him by surprise. I had a friend who gave me a copy of *When Your Dreams Die*. She was a friend who I met at college, and she was there for me when I needed to cry, vent, pray, and talk. She was such a good friend at a most crucial point of my life; I knew God brought her into my life. She is now my wife, with whom I serve the Lord.

The aim of this book, and particularly this section on suicide, is to help us understand the ways we can help the bereaved and recognize the hindrances to healing. I asked my friends to share particular acts and words that helped them or that didn't help them work through their grief. Here are some of their responses:

- Some friends called or dropped by and allowed us to talk and share memories and sadness. Also, I attended a suicide support group in 1989, which helped me.

- Helping others and being more compassionate has also helped me.

- Some helped with housework, cooked dinner, watched the other kids, ran errands, and best of all, just listened or held me when I was crying.

- Just showing up for the Shiva was helpful, sending cards, donating money to charity, and planting trees in his name. My rabbi told me "Suicide is the last powerful act of the powerless." I like that statement.

- God graciously used people from the church I was attending to minister to me and my mom. My pastor was caring and was available for us when we were ready to talk.

I also asked some families to share what consequences of their loss were the hardest to accept and here's what they listed:

- The fact that I will have no more children.

- I'll never be a grandmother.

- Guilt that I contributed to his suicide.

- This may have been preventable, and it may have been an accidental suicide.

- He'll never meet my wife or kids.

- He won't see me graduate from college or know of my calling as a pastor.

- He won't see me live clean and sober.

- He only had a brief glimpse of the transformation Christ did in my life.

My friends also shared with me what was *not* helpful:

- Some people just wanted to move on and talk about their problems, which seemed so trivial to me at the time.

- It didn't help when people said, "I know what you're going through."

- Some watched me too closely or followed me around when what I really needed was time for myself.

- People did not come to us and allow us to speak and grieve, which made us feel neglected.

- Well-intentioned folks from my church would try to comfort me by telling me, "God works all things for the good of those who love Him."

Though Christians undoubtedly mean well when they share Romans 8:28, they must be careful to avoid being insensitive, as this response shows:

How was any good going to come out of this? This was my golfing partner, my fishing buddy. We would go crabbing on Barnegat Bay in the summer time. My dad took me all over the country and the world with him before I was 16 years old. How was this going to work for the good?

A woman who called me when I was a guest on a radio talk show expressed a fear that often eats away at the suicide survivors. Lillian's granddaughter had died by suicide just a year earlier when she was 23. Lillian sobbed as she said, "My Christian friends have told me that I will never see my granddaughter again because since she died by suicide, she will not go to heaven."

My first reaction was outrage. How could anyone possibly think it was necessary to say that to Lillian now that her granddaughter was dead? What purpose would it serve?

I asked, "Lillian, was your granddaughter a Christian?"

She replied, "Oh, yes, I led her to Christ myself. I know she was a Christian."

I answered, "From what I read in Scripture, the basis upon which we will be admitted into heaven is whether we have received Christ as our personal Savior, not on how we died. If your granddaughter received Jesus Christ as her personal Savior, I believe you will see her again when you arrive in heaven." As we continued talking, I could hear the relief in Lillian's voice.

Since that time, I have studied Scripture very closely to make sure I gave Lillian the right answer. The Bible mentions five completed suicides: Samson, Saul, Ahitophel, Zimri, and Judas

Iscariot. The Bible teaches that Samson and Saul were leaders appointed by the Lord, and they belonged to God. I have not been able to find any Scriptures to indicate that their position with God changed after their suicides. They were still His children. Because Jesus implied that Judas would not be in heaven, many have felt Jesus' statement referred to Judas' suicide, which they conclude is the unpardonable sin. But if Judas will not be in heaven, the reason is that he was not willing to acknowledge Jesus as the Christ and not that he died by suicide.

Suicide is the murder of self. The Bible teaches we should not kill another human being. Yet we see examples in the Bible of people being forgiven of murder. David, Moses, and Paul come to mind. In the event of suicide, the person usually would not have had time to ask God's forgiveness of that particular sin before he died, but that could be true of other types of deaths as well. If God could forgive murder of others, how could He not forgive self-murder?

No one could possibly understand suicide more than God Himself because He knows our thoughts and understands why someone would think suicide is the best thing for him. Surely God's compassion and forgiveness are available to a Christian whose mind has become confused and depressed. Also, many of us will undoubtedly come to our Father with some sin still unconfessed, but we are still God's children if we have invited Him into our lives.

> My sheep hear my voice, and I know them, and they follow me: And I give unto them eternal life; and they shall never perish, neither shall any man pluck them out of my hand. My Father, which gave them me, is greater than all; and no man is able to pluck them out of my Father's hand (John 10:27-29).

I hesitated to write this section for fear some would misunderstand and quote me as saying to die by suicide is not wrong. I have not said that. Suicide is sin. It's as wrong as murder, rape, or any other violent crime, and those who die by suicide will have to face the Lord Jesus Christ with their sin just as the rest of us will have to with ours. However, nothing in Scripture depicts suicide as the unpardonable sin.

I'm not writing this as a theologian but simply as a woman who sees the hearts that are broken because a family member died by suicide. These families need our constant support and understanding as we patiently lead them to forgive others—and themselves.

Survivors of suicide often experience a greater sense of helplessness, anger, and guilt than those who have lost a loved one in an accident or through an illness. I asked several parents what they wish they had known or understood before their child completed suicide.

- I wish I had more time with him. We were estranged for 18 years! He reconciled with me just six months before he died.

- I wish I had known he was severely depressed.

- If I could turn back the clock, I would have been more aware of his surroundings and thoughts.

Regarding his father's suicide Mike told me, "If I was around as my dad's depression deepened and his alcohol use increased, when it seemed that the weight of the world was on his shoulders and he could find no way out from under it, I would have told him I loved him more than I had told him. I would have talked more about the time we came in first place in the golf league. I would have prayed for him and the situation he was dealing with at his machine shop."

After reading the two appendixes on losing someone to AIDS or by suicide, I hope you have made some observations:

- Many needs of the bereaved, regardless of how a loved one died, are the same as those of others who have experienced the death of a loved one by any other cause. We need someone to listen to us, cry with us, and give us room to grieve.

- In addition, we need to be extra sensitive that we do not add guilt to the family.

- We need to make sure the family feels totally accepted and in no way stigmatized because of how their loved one died.

- Once a person has died, the cause of death should be of little or no importance to us as Christians.

- Healing from a loss by death takes much longer than any of us expect, and when death is by suicide, AIDS, or any other violent means, healing may take even longer. We need to give the bereaved all of the time they need. Remember, *grief takes as long as it takes.*

I recently had the opportunity to speak to a group of counselors regarding how to counsel the bereaved. I asked Mike if he would be willing to be my "counselee" so that I could demonstrate my approach to a bereaved person. Mike's father had died by suicide more than 14 years prior to our time together. Mike readily agreed to help me.

My time with Mike was one of the most moving times I can recall as a speaker. As I asked Mike to share his story, I think even Mike was shocked at how near the surface his tears were. The rest of the counseling staff were soon passing around the tissues. Mike clearly understood what caused his father to choose suicide, but we all could still feel Mike's pain even 14 years later.

Then I asked, "If you could talk to your dad today, what would you say to him?" After many tears, Mike said, "I would say 'I love you, and I forgive you.'"

After a death, the survivors often need to gradually move toward forgiveness. In the event of a violent crime, the family has to deal with the perpetrator. Please understand that forgiveness does not mean we release a person from his responsibility, we won't press charges, we don't expect restitution, or we condone the act. But forgiveness removes feelings of vengeance, resolves anger that may consume us, allows us to leave the problem in God's hands, and permits us to proceed in our healing process.

We must forgive ourselves when we have inadvertently caused a death. Several times I have listened to the stories of heartbroken people who accidentally caused the death of a friend or family member. Their pain is cruelly intense, and they continue to bear enormous guilt feelings. These people must receive strong support from other family members and from their friends. Whether the guilt is real or imagined, professional counseling for the survivor is vital. He probably will have to talk out the events repeatedly with his family and and others involved in the tragedy. As he gets help and is able to voice his feelings of guilt and remorse without fear of condemnation, he will eventually be able to forgive himself, and in time, his pain will heal.

People also need to forgive when the death of a family member from AIDS or suicide has brought shame, reproach, and other negative reactions to them and their family. They can eventually experience the freedom Mike describes:

> As I look back, now 15 years removed from Dad's suicide, God seems more intimate to me. You see, although God was aware of my dad's decision to seek a permanent solution to a temporary problem, his death broke God's heart just as it did mine and my family's. When God seemed furthest from me, He was actually closest to me. He sent His people and most

of all Carole, my wife, my way to help me through the grieving process. I think I'll always grieve my dad's death; I know I'll never forget it. But just as the ripples of water grow farther apart and slower in their frequency, God is showing and has shown what a "new normal" looks like.

Notes

The Rose of Sorrow

1. This quote is generally credited to Sir James Barrie, the author of *Peter Pan*.

The Rose of Forgiveness

1. S.I. McMillen, MD., *None of These Diseases* (Westwood, NJ: Fleming H. Revell Company, 1963), 73-74.

2. Lewis B. Smedes, "Forgiveness: Healing the Hurts We Don't Deserve," *Family Life Today*, January 1985, 24-28.

3. Joni Eareckson Tada and Steve Estes, *A Step Further* (Grand Rapids, Michigan: Zondervan Publishing House, 1978), 15-16.

The Rose of Remembrance

1. Joseph Bayly, *The Last Thing We Talk About* (Elgin, IL: David C. Cook Publishing Co., 1973), 66.

The Rose of Innocence

1. Janice C. Harris, ACSW-CSW, and Angela Bennett, "Helping Children Cope with Death in the Family" (Hurst, Texas: Mothers Against Drunk Drivers, 1984, pamphlet).

The Rose of Uniqueness

1. Florence Littauer, *Personality Plus* (Old Tappan, New Jersey: Fleming H. Revell, 1983), 18-20.

2. Ibid.

3. Ibid.

4. Ibid.

5. Lana Bateman, *Personality Patterns* (Dallas, Texas: Philippian Ministries, 1985), 3-12.

6. Chart compiled by Marilyn Heavilin from her own material and material presented in *Personality Puzzle* (Grand Rapids, MI: Fleming H. Revell, 1992). Permission granted by CLASS Services, Inc. For further information on this topic, call 800-433-6633.

The Rose of Tenderness

1. Robert L. Veninga, "How to Cope with Heartache," *Ladies Home Journal*, November 1985, 74-82.

The Rose of Farewells

1. Tom Griggs, "A mystery solved," *Redlands Daily Facts* (Redlands, CA, August 21, 1997), 1.

2. Ibid.

3. Ibid.

Other Excellent
Harvest House Reading

WHEN LIFE IS CHANGED FOREVER
Rick Taylor. In 1979, Taylor lost his five-year-old son in a drowning accident. With candor, Taylor speaks to wounded hearts about the agony of empty arms and the raging of the soul in the aftermath of death.

0-89081-971-8

THE FATHER HEART OF GOD
Floyd McClung. McClung freshly reveals how discovering God as the perfectly reliable, perfectly compassionate Father—eager to meet every need, ready to give His love—brings freedom and healing from deep emotional wounds. Includes study guide.

0-7369-1215-0

HELPING YOUR KIDS DEAL WITH ANGER, FEAR, AND SADNESS
H. Norman Wright. No parent likes to see thier child struggle, especially with dark emotions like anger, fear, and depression. Family counselor Norm Wright helps parents understand these intense moods and develop sound principles in dealing effectively with them.

0-7369-1333-5

LETTER TO A GRIEVING HEART
Billy Sprague, photography by John MacMurray. With compassion and perspective, Billy Sprague shares personal insights and encouragement with those living through grief and heartache. The hope-filled photographs of nature and insightful text assure readers that they will feel the sun again.

0-7369-0732-7

HELP ME TRUST YOU, LORD

Emilie Barnes with Anne Christian Buchanan. In this follow-up to *Fill My Cup, Lord,* Emilie gently reminds readers that it is during "the valley of the shadow" times that we come to know the abundant reality of God's presence.

0-7369-0246-5

WHY DO BAD THINGS HAPPEN IF GOD IS GOOD?

Ron Rhodes. Bible scholar Ron Rhodes addresses the problem of pain with the heart of a pastor and the mind of an apologist. Ron explores the unshakable biblical truths that provide a strong foundation in stormy times.

0-7369-1296-7